Flower Fabrications

Flower Fabrications

*Forty hand fashioned flowers
to create including silk tulips,
organdy roses, gingham cornflowers
and crepe paper daisies*

JEAN WILKINSON
with Katharyn Duff

Butterick Publishing

PHOTOGRAPHY

Ralph Leone: Color Plates 1, 2, 4, 5, 6, 7, 9, 10, 11, 13, 15, 16

Bob Stoller for FAMILY CIRCLE Magazine: Color Plates 3, 8, 12, 14

ILLUSTRATIONS

Jan Walker

BOOK DESIGN

Betty Binns

Copyright © 1977 by
Butterick Publishing
161 Sixth Avenue
New York, New York 10013

A Division of American Can Company

Library of Congress Catalog Card Number 76-26364
International Standard Book Number 0-88421-025-1

Printed in the U.S.A.
First Printing, October 1976
Second Printing, October 1977

Contents

Acknowledgments

When the opportunity to do this book came along, right after I said, "Yes, I'd love to do that," I began to ponder "why" I could say yes so quickly when I so obviously would need help. Why could I so readily accept such a challenge without even a thought as to "whether" I could? It is because I am one of those fortunate people who can so depend on my family and my friends that I am able to say "Yes" without even blinking. That is an asset for which I am extremely grateful.

Even so, could I possibly get all those flowers made and photographed and still be able to communicate flower fashioning techniques into book form in the allotted time? Doubt.

As I most likely do when I have doubts, I prayed about it. Then I thought of Katharyn Duff, as I had so many times over the last 30 years. Katharyn was my high school journalism teacher for six weeks on her way to a career in newspapering. I had many times longed to be reacquainted with her. I knew she was the assistant editor of the *Abilene Reporter-News* in the city downstate, near where I was reared.

I wondered if there were a chance she might consider helping me get my thoughts on flowers into book form. I decided to call her and see. "Katharyn, this is Jean Wilkinson in Amarillo. You don't know me but ..." She interrupted me with, "Well, I wish I did!" and that was all I needed. Certainly I could arrange that. And I did.

Katharyn and I have done this book together. Now understand, Katharyn has never made a flower in her life and I would be much surprised if she ever does. She is a historian, not a flower maker. But she herself blooms daily for thousands of readers through her column, "Page One," in the *Reporter-News*. The experience has been priceless to me, and I am certain Katharyn has enjoyed it also. She is an extraordinary woman, always eager for a new venture. And venture it was. As I designed and made flowers, I would tape my ideas, my thoughts and the how-tos and send them to her. It was her task to keep me organized and prepare the text. No small feat!

I am deeply thankful for my reacquaintance with Katharyn Duff and for her help on this book. I am equally grateful to each of the following people whose help I took for granted when I said, "Yes, I'd love to do that." My friends and my family . . . these are the real blossoms of my life . . . those who make it possible for me to fashion flowers.

🌸 Dick and Glenna Brooks, who have so encouraged my faith that I am confident to share my abilities.

🌸 Ralph Leone, for unlimited patience with me and for his sensitivity to what I wanted in photography.

🌸 Jan Walker, for her ability to illustrate the how-tos with seldom a question.

🌸 Deborah Harding, editor of Creative Crafts and Needlework for *Family Circle Magazine*, who has for several years encouraged, prodded, coached and coaxed me to make better and better flowers. My thanks, also, to Art Hettich, editor of *Family Circle*, who permitted me to republish some of my work previously published by his magazine.

🌸 Theo Taylor, for constant encouragement and responding to my every need.

🌸 Ann Neale, for her efficient typing.

🌸 Charlotte Quackenbush, Dusty McGuire and Margie Bast, who arranged flowers for photographs.

🌸 Mr. and Mrs. Keith Taylor and Mr. and Mrs. George Lokey for allowing me to photograph flowers in their homes and Jim Remy, who allowed me to photograph in his store, Concord House.

🌸 Mary Schmidt, Margie Bast and my mother, Roxie Curb, who spent many hours making flowers for photographs.

Beth Duff, Helen and Alvin Seibt and their daughters, Mary Helen and Betty Kay, for technical help . . . and for hours of good humor and hospitality.

My sister, Bettejane De Vasto, her husband Frank, and their family, whose opinions I have always treasured.

All of the Wilkinsons, my husband's family, who have always supported me in everything.

Thank you all,
JEAN WILKINSON

INTRODUCTION

How to Use This Book

This book is designed and written for use. Its purpose is to instruct you in the art of making flowers—if necessary, to persuade, inspire, cajole and coax you to try your hand at this "so elegant an employment." That expression, "so elegant . . . ," is one describing this art found in *Godey's Lady's Book,* published in 1847. Translated into today's vernacular it means that flower fashioning is an excellent, a splendid hobby.

Glance, if you will, through the pages to get a feeling for the content in this book. The approach is to "begin with the beginning." First, there is an introduction to this art form, along with some reasons you should try it. Next comes a reference chapter, "Basics for Bouquets." Here you will find generalized information on essential tools and procedures. Familiarize yourself with these before you begin your work—and know you will become more familiar as you continue fashioning flowers. This chapter will answer questions which may arise later. After this, come the "flower chapters."

Each of the chapters on flowers stands alone. For example, if you are disinterested in buttercups and daisies, the first offered, skip them and go directly to those blossoms which attract you. Each flower comes with its own instructions. You need not progress chapter by chapter.

"A Better Buttercup" is the first of the flower chapters. The blossoms given here are simple to make, and are of a simple material, crepe paper. From there we will go into the fabrics, the cottons, silks, sheers and the velvets and then the "Unlikely Etceteras." The Etceteras, made with unusual materials, require more time to make than do most others in the book. There is a chapter on flowers for a special occasion, a wedding. There is one on pot plants and, finally, one on displaying the flowers you have handcrafted.

The book has some features you might notice. Patterns are printed life-size on color pages. No need to scale them and easy to find. Each flower how-to section begins with "A memo to Flower Fashioners." This is a key to the chapter on "Basics for Bouquets," giving pages for instructions which fit the techniques used in that flower. And each flower chapter begins with a line drawing of the color plates showing the flowers completed.

This book is to be put to your use. Perhaps it will be your introduction, your initiation into a hobby which is both satisfying and splendid—flower fashioning.

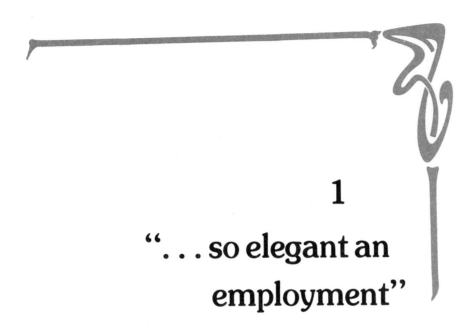

1

"... so elegant an employment"

The first flower I ever made must have been dreadful.

A merciful memory clouds the details of my childish effort, but I think it was supposed to be a buttercup, dainty and graceful as those soft yellow lovelies which pop up in West Texas pastures in late spring. I know I was copying some sort of wild posy because my mother grew children, not flowers, in our backyard. Any gardening time was devoted to such practical plants as tomatoes and black-eyed peas.

I know, too, that my first flower was contrived of materials at hand, small scraps of fabric, a piece of a coat hanger, flour paste, bits of crepe paper pocketed in wads and brought home from an exciting May Day program at school. In a household with eight children, on a dry-land farm during a regional drought and a national depression, we made do with what we had.

"Celebration of the ordinary," so someone described the life style we learned from necessity and by parental teaching. We assumed then that ours was a deprived way of living, but I can see now we were very fortunate. As children we had to develop an awareness of the usual — and imagination of its potential. Empty thread spools were wheels for a matchbox freight train, or they were longhorn cattle for a make-believe roundup. Around the farm there were birds' nests to spy on and wonder at. Did the colors of the eggs help mama birds identify their own? There were wild flowers, too, and that day I had copied one.

... Flower making ... so elegant an employment.

GODEY'S LADY'S BOOK, 1847

Flowers are words which even a babe can understand.

BISHOP COXE

15

Even I, looking at my creation, could see that Mother Nature would not be envious. The petals drooped, limp and formless. The stem was chrysanthemum-size. The green crepe paper was bunched over blobs of paste which held it to the coat-hanger wire. But my heart knew what I had intended if my fingers did not. And when I displayed it, holding it upside down for the sake of those spineless petals, my mother guessed right off that it was a flower. As mothers can, she even found some words of praise.

Praise! That is one of the rewards for fashioning flowers. Compliments! Who doesn't enjoy compliments? They boost our confidence. Desire for the approval of others is a human craving and a healthy one. So is the nobler urge to create. Our response to this urge to "do" or to "make" affects our relations with others. The urge is satisfied in a joyful way when we create a "thing of beauty" such as a hand-fashioned flower. We look at it and know it is lovely. It is no plastic blob, no cooky-cutter, look-alike, artificial facsimile, but an original bit of art. We made it! Its loveliness will endure, pleasing others as well as ourselves.

A thing of beauty is a joy forever . . . It will never pass into nothingness.

KEATS

The activities we term hobbies, those creative activities in which we engage for the pleasure of the doing, divide roughly into two categories. There are the crafts which were in earlier civilizations necessities to feed and house and clothe the family and make it more comfortable—woodworking, pottery, quilting, soap-making and the like. Then there are the less utilitarian, the more artistic efforts, which feed the soul and add meaning, beauty, and understanding to life.

Nowadays it is often difficult to distinguish the two. When the machine age came along, the old useful crafts were no longer essential to every household. Strangely, however, they did not die away. People still enjoyed doing them. Techniques and materials improved. The old crafts have in many instances become new artistry.

Flower in the crannied wall . . . if I could understand what you are . . . I should know what God and man is.

TENNYSON

Flower fashioning is a craft with the charm of both the useful and the artistic categories. Through the ages the flower has been a favorite subject as man has tried to capture and copy its beauty. Creative art represents man's efforts to imitate God's wonders, to interpret them to himself and to others. I think we can see this when art is reduced to its simplest form: the toddler with crayons and paper drawing a sunset, a bird, a sketch of home or of someone he loves. Expand art to its most magnificent form: the sculptor, painter, poet would explain Truth. The flower is for all times and for all people the essential luxury. It serves prince and peasant alike, decorating his world. It is the universal symbol of beauty. We need flowers, need them growing on the hillside, blooming at the doorway, or delivered from the florist's shop. Alas, fresh flowers are too often denied us by circumstances.

16

Before there was a floral industry, anyone who wanted flowers out of season had to make them. Their artistic efforts thus served a useful purpose. Handmade flowers decorated stately colonial mansions and rough frontier cabins alike. Crocheted flowers adorned our grandmother's otherwise drab frocks. And land sakes alive! The scandalous way brazen young ladies would pin tiny satin rosebuds to garters, even to unmentionable undergarments!

The fashioning of flowers fits even better into today's civilization. Urban and suburban routines often leave little time for flower gardening. The apartment dweller usually has no space for a hollyhock much less for a bed of roses. Advances in transportation have made all blossoms in season at all times in all places, but fresh flowers are still a short-lived and costly luxury most of us reserve for special occasions. Yet flowers are an important accessory, along with books and pictures, to give a home personality and charm. A pot of geraniums here, a bunch of violets there, a dramatic arrangement for the foyer, roses for the dining table ... flowers are the jewelry of a well-dressed life.

So fashion your own.

As I felt about my first flower so I feel about my latest. Oh, I can still make a flower which disappoints me so that my joy in accomplishment is tempered somewhat by adult recognition of imperfection. But this "elegant employment" is bound by no hard and fast rules. It produces no real "losers," only challenges for improvement or hints of whole new ideas and techniques. Your pansy or day lily may or may not be an exact copy of one pictured in this book or in an encyclopedia. No matter. Precise uniformity in flowers is not a virtue. Your variation may have nothing to do with the quality of your creation. Perhaps my flower is not "better" than yours, only different, and that is okay. You and I would not paint identical pictures. And find, if you have unlimited time, identical blossoms in a garden.

The fashioning of flowers is satisfying and satisfactory because you do not have to conform to any set of rules. It can be a simple or a sophisticated undertaking depending on your objective or your mood. Materials can be exotic or commonplace. What pleases you? A pink satin rose? Unpretentious paper daisies? Perhaps you are in the mood for velvet violets, provocative and romantic, or something as wry and carefree as a Mexican caricature of nature. This is a feel-free handicraft done best when you let your imagination ramble. It is done best when you shake loose any "I can't" feeling and begin to experiment with new materials, different methods, ideas I have not even thought to suggest here. Learn not to be discouraged by those efforts which "Mother Nature would not envy." After all, that old gal starts over every spring. Try again, using cotton velvet rather than rayon

How does the meadow flower its bloom unfold?

Because the lovely little flower is free down to its roots, and in that freedom, bold.

WORDSWORTH

17

Flowers have the objectless, spontaneous luxury of existence that belongs to childhood.

GODEY'S LADY'S BOOK, 1850

ribbon for a calyx. When you thus free yourself to experiment you become less inhibited by mistakes. You will find that some errors will, to your amazement, turn into happy accidents. Then flower fashioning is fun, exciting, what it should be.

I should warn you, however, that making flowers can be a preoccupying pastime. Become engrossed in a flower project which is going well and your first thought of dinner strikes when you hear a hungry family coming in from work or play. To avoid such crises I sometimes use a trick I learned from an Erma Bombeck column. As I start work I put an onion in the oven and turn the heat on low. When the family storms in asking, "When's dinner?" the aroma at least suggests food is on the way as I fake it from there. Or, you might prefer a ruse used by a friend of mine. She burns vanilla candles while she works and her family thinks she has been baking all afternoon when she brings out the lately thawed dessert.

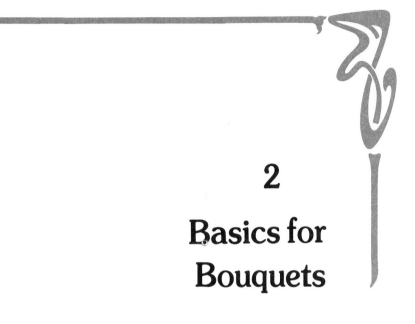

2

Basics for Bouquets

The best site and the best time for your flower fashioning depends on your house and on your household. In this hobby, as in others, that comes first. A bit of planning before you begin helps. No matter what attempts I make to "get organized," there are times when I feel akin to a character in a little book by Shi Beck, one who said she didn't lead her life, she chased around "trying to catch it."

You should select for your flower making a room with certain accommodations. You will need quick access to sink and running water, these to care for dye and for hand washing—you must approach flower making with clean hands and keep them clean. Choose a spot which will provide counter space or a table top of comfortable height. It will not take much space, but it should be in an area you can set aside while you tend to other chores. If you cherish your reputation as a housekeeper, select a corner generally off-limits to guests. Careful, though. Isolating yourself often makes others in your household feel neglected. If you have small children, select a nook where the floor is easily cleaned. You will let the youngsters "help" at times and that means they will be dropping pieces of fabric glue-side-down. Find a spot which affords some drawer or cabinet area to store tools and materials. And, finally, you will at times need access to an oven and to an ironing board for quick-drying fabrics and for adding finishing touches.

All the needs for my flower fashioning are in a corner of my kitchen.

19

Here the sink, oven, cabinet, ironing board, and counter space are handy. The kitchen is in-bounds for my husband and our teen-age son and for intimate friends. Just off the kitchen is an informal family room where we often eat together. There is a pool table which, since mine is a very tolerant family, is often laden with flower materials; and here is the television set to which my guys stay glued during football season. From the kitchen I can feel I am a part of their conversation, can fetch snacks during commercials, can join in the celebration when the Dallas Cowboys do something spectacular.

Now, the time for your project. Block off at least an hour, better two, for a flower session. Assemble tools and supplies in advance. If you have to stop, dress, and drive to the shop for the right size wire, you will surely run into Aunt Min whom you have not seen for too long. She will likely invite you to lunch and there goes your flower time. Plan ahead.

All the tools and supplies I suggest here are not necessary for each and every individual project. I will list them all at once, however. There is one simple rule for you to follow: use whatever works! Many of these tools are already in your home or apartment. If not, try the neighborhood hardware, discount, variety, hobby, fabric store, or floral supply shop. They are not expensive, even with inflation.

Tools and Supplies

Aluminum wrap The lightweight grade is fine for ordinary work. Use heavier grades for flowers such as poppies and roses.

Bleach For removing color in decorations.

Bread dough See page 31.

Brushes Keep a variety of sizes on hand. I use dime-store watercolor brushes for delicate art work such as "bleeding" colors and decorating certain petals. Larger brushes, ½" to 1½", are for sizing fabrics and for applying varnish used in some projects. See illustration 1. For years I avoided varnishes and oil paints because I hated cleaning my brushes every time I used them. One day some kind soul pointed out an obvious solution. He said to keep brushes soft I should store them temporarily in one-pound coffee cans, the sort with plastic lids. Pour several inches of turpentine into the can and stick the handle of the brush through a slit in the lid so the bristles can dangle into the turpentine. Be sure the bristles are submerged but do not touch bottom. Brushes will remain constantly usable without further tending. Of course, keep the turpentine stored in a cabinet away from heat and out of children's reach. See illustration 2.

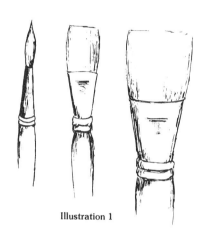

Illustration 1

Illustration 2

Cans and jars   Save yourself a supply. They are handy for storing bits and pieces.

Cardboard   Lightweight, such as the bottom and top of a dress box will serve; you need cardboard for tracing patterns.

Dyes   See page 27.

Fabrics   If you are a seamstress, your scrap bag is a treasure chest. If not, try the fabric store. You will find that very few fabrics are 100 per cent "anything." Most are mixtures, blends with synthetics. I will try to give you the mixtures I find successful. Many bindings, ruffling materials and decorative trims will work beautifully into flowers. See illustration 3. Understand, I do not walk myself to death hunting a specific hue or shade of fabric. In many instances I buy white materials and dye them as explained on page 27.

Most fabrics are woven with obvious threads going back and forth, both horizontally and vertically. These obvious straight lines of thread are referred to as the "grain" or the "weave" or the "straight" of the fabric. Very often in cutting petals and leaves from fabric, it will be to the advantage of the flower to cut the pattern on the "bias." This means that you place the pattern diagonally across the weave at approximately a 45 degree angle. This provides an ability to stretch and pull the edges of the petal or leaf to effect a dimensional look rather than the appearance of a flat piece of fabric.

Illustration 3

I cannot tell you specifically how much material you should buy for what. That will be determined by the number of flowers you want to make and by the width of the fabric you select. The most accurate way of estimating yardage is to, first, determine the width of the fabric you intend to use. Then, tape together newspapers to equal this width. Lay the patterns for one flower onto the newspaper, being careful to note at what angle the pattern should be laid for cutting. This is indicated on the pattern by an arrow directing you to place the arrow on the "straight" of the fabric. Finally, multiply the amount of fabric required to make one flower by the number of flowers you will make.

Felt-tip markers   These you will use and use. Collect them in all colors you can find. They will be used primarily for special effects of coloration in decorating certain flowers. Felt-tip markers come in two varieties. One is the water-base marker whose colors can be diluted or removed with water. The other is the alcohol or "permanent" base whose colors can be diluted or removed with alcohol, nail polish remover and with some petroleum-based products. Most petroleum-based products such as varnish will produce a "running" of colors, an advantage in certain types of flowers, particularly those made of paper and metals. I prefer to use the permanent markers simply because they are just that. Their color is easily controlled with rubbing alcohol and they seem to fade less quickly. Water-soluble markers, however, come in a wider range of colors and are also satisfactory to use. However, any contact of the flower with moisture such as glue may cause uncontrolled running of colors. When buying markers, read the labels to know if they are water-soluble or permanent. If the label does not say, test it first to determine whether moisture will smear its markings. If so, it is likely water-soluble. Always keep markers capped when not in use, otherwise ink will evaporate. Both fine line pens and blunt pointed heavy markers are possible decorating tools, depending on the requirements of the flowers. See illustration 4.

Illustration 4

Floral ribbon   This is a great material for fashioning long and spiky leaves such as many bulb-type flowers have. I often use it when I need a leaf with wire support between two layers. The ribbon, available at floral shops and at many variety and hobby shops, comes in about the right widths so there is little waste. It can be bought in various shades of green and it may be of satin or velvet finish. I often use contrasting fabrics in the blossom and the leaf of a flower, velvet leaves with a satin flower, shiny leaves with a flower whose petals have a dull finish. The contrast in texture and shade is complementary.

Floral tape   See page 27.

Fusible webbing   A translucent web of fibers that fuse with the heat of an iron to join two layers of fabric together. Is available in fabric stores.

Glue   The nicest thing which ever happened to flower fashioning. See page 26.

Ice pick   A convenient tool, as any housewife, hobbyist, or craftsman well knows. See illustration 5.

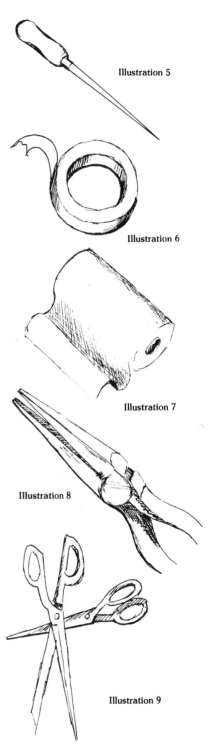

Illustration 5

Illustration 6

Illustration 7

Illustration 8

Illustration 9

Iron   Necessary to remove wrinkles from fabrics before placing and cutting patterns. Also used to achieve special effects such as "crinkling" for certain flowers.

Masking tape   The ¾″ is the handiest, but any size will do. If the roll is too wide, simply tear off the right size strip. I invariably use masking tape at some point in assembling a blossom and a stem. It seems to give me comfort to know the flower will stay together. See illustration 6.

Paper toweling   For blotting excess sizing off materials—and for the "oops!" moment when there is a spill. See illustration 7.

Plastic wrap   A bit of this between the glue jar and the lid will keep the two from adhering.

Pliers   If you do not have a pair of needle-nosed pliers, invest in one. Snub-nosed pliers are good for bending heavy wire, but you will find the needle-nose serves you better. See illustration 8.

Razor blade   Single-edge fits for many a job.

Rubbing alcohol   To be used combined with felt-tip markers for decorating petals. See page 33.

Ruler or tape measure   Any sort will do, but a steel-edged ruler is a helpful tool.

Scissors   The seamstress knows that two pairs are needed: one for cutting fabrics and the other for cutting paper and other materials. Never should the twain be mixed. Marking the scissors with a colored felt-tip marker will help identify them at a glance. See illustration 9.

Sizing board   This will be used in sizing fabrics. A large breadboard will serve, if available. If not, have the lumberyard or your favorite handyman cut a piece of ½″ or ¾″ plywood about 18″ by 24″. Whatever the wood, it should be soft enough that thumb tacks for fastening the fabric will push into it easily. Lightly sand the board so that fabric will not snag.

Thumb tacks or push pins   Use these for fastening fabric to sizing board.

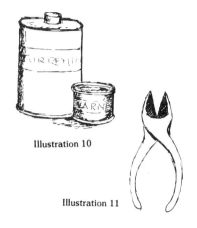

Illustration 10

Illustration 11

Tissue paper   Any sort which is transparent enough to use in tracing patterns will serve. Even a piece of wrapping from a new pair of shoes will do.

Turpentine   For storing and cleaning brushes when using varnishes. And remember children—store both out of their reach. See illustration 10.

Varnish   Some flowers call for several coats of clear, fast-drying varnish. A small can will do in the beginning of your work. See illustration 10.

Wire   See page 26.

Wire cutters Most pliers, including the needle-nosed ones, have cutters on them, but I prefer the big side-cutters because they are heavier, easier to use, and make a much cleaner cut. See illustration 11. Many department stores and mail-order catalogs have them, as well as lumberyards, hobby shops, and the like.

The Glossary

Before we begin, it occurs to me we should be together on each other's language about flowers and flower making. Flower parts are shown in illustration 12. Other words and terms I use are:

Beard   The fuzzy throat of an iris. See illustration 13.

Bleed   To make colors mix or "run" to create artistic effects. See illustration 14.

Calyx   The cup-shaped, leaflike base on which a flower rests, usually green, sometimes of no great importance after the blossom has opened. See illustration 12 and 15.

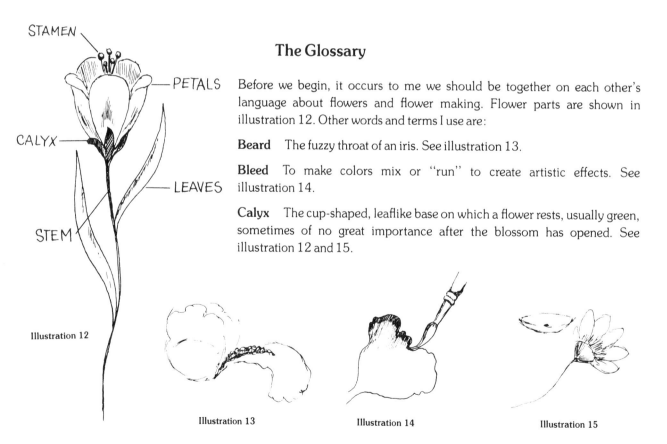

Illustration 12

Illustration 13

Illustration 14

Illustration 15

Center   The middle area of a flower. I usually refer to the flower's "center" when there is no identifiable stamen.

Crimp   To press into small regular ridges or indentations, as the edge of a petal or leaf to achieve a special effect.

Crinkle   To make wrinkles or ripples in the fabric or paper. Can be done with fingers or, in some instances, with a hot iron. See illustration 16.

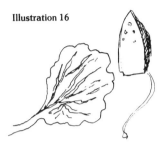

Illustration 16

Flute   To make a wavy edge as in a pie crust. See illustration 17.

Fringe   Edging, usually decorative and often ornate. Often done by slitting fabric with scissors in a very close pattern. See illustration 18.

Leaves   Foliage, usually green, sometimes distinctive as in a geranium or a nasturtium, sometimes not. See illustration 12. In fashioning flowers you do not always attempt to make yours a carbon copy of the original. When making a flower whose leaf is not distinctive, I often use a different leaf shape simply to benefit the total arrangement.

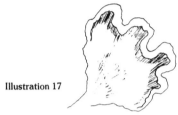

Illustration 17

Pleat   A fold made by doubling the material on itself. See illustration 19.

Score   To make indentations with a sharp instrument such as the point of scissors or a metal cuticle implement or an ice pick. Usually done on the back side of sized fabrics such as velvet and especially effective to suggest subtle leaf veins. See illustration 20.

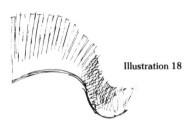

Illustration 18

Size   See page 28.

Speckle   To decorate or "freckle" with dots.

Stamen   The center part, inside the ring of petals, sometimes a negligible part of the flower, in some instances distinctive, a focal point. See illustration 12.

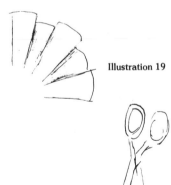

Illustration 19

Trumpet   The center crown of a daffodil. See illustration 21.

Veins   The branching framework of a leaf. See illustration 22.

Illustration 22

Illustration 21

Illustration 20

25

Essentials in Flower Fashioning

In flower fashioning there are certain standard materials, procedures, and ways of assembling and decorating your finished product. Let me give you these in more or less outline form.

First, other than the contents of the blossom itself, there are four essential materials: glue, wire, masking tape, and floral tape.

GLUE

White glues are essential. You will need two strengths, regular and quick-sticking or "heavy" glue.

More of the regular glue is required because you will use it in sizing and also in making bread dough. I use plain white Slomon's Sobo fabric glue for this. It does not get brittle with age as will some other glues. Whatever brand you choose, experiment with it first to be sure it will do what you want it to. The quick-sticking glue is, on the other hand, for "sticking something to something," as a petal to a rosebud, a wire to a piece of fabric. It holds quickly, making your work less tedious. Quick-sticking glue, while you do not use a great deal of it, is the one most called for in instructions on flower fashioning.

I repeat, regular glue is for sizing or bonding two pieces of fabric together to make a leaf or petal because it spreads much easier than does the quick-sticking. Quick-sticking glue is for assembling blossoms.

WIRE

Another necessary element is wire. You will often use two, perhaps three, wires in your flower: a heavier wire for the stem, a lighter wire or wires for support to control petals and the leaf.

It is usually necessary that the lighter wire be covered. You may cover it yourself (see page 31). You can also buy it already covered, which I do except when I need special colors. The wire, called "thread-covered wire," can be purchased in green, sometimes in white and in other colors. Usually it can be found in the hobby shop or you may order it from Lee Wards, Elgin, Illinois 60120, or from American Handicrafts, 1011 Focha, Fort Worth, Texas 76107. If the color you need is not available, purchase white and dye it.

Remember, wire is measured in "gauges," a measurement of the diameter. See illustration 23. The larger the gauge number, the thinner the wire. As one point of reference, the average coat hanger is about #12 to #14 gauge. This is about right for the stem of a very large flower. For most

Illustration 23

flowers, I use #16 gauge wire which is slightly lighter weight than a coat hanger. For a smaller, more delicate flower, you will want a larger number (finer wire) such as a #20 gauge. For support wire I very often use #22 or #24 gauge. Wire is usually available in 18″ lengths at hobby stores, floral shops and the like. Very fine wire can be purchased by the spool at variety or hardware stores.

Another point about wire: I always use a piece of #16 gauge about 4″ long to apply quick-sticking glue to wires and such. It's always close at hand, disposable, and seems to serve well in spreading the heavy glue.

MASKING TAPE

Masking tape has become to me almost as important as glue in making flowers. Its function is primarily for assembling flowers—adding insurance that the twisted petals will stay together; that the flower head will remain secure to the stem wire.

It also serves to smooth over a bumpy stem of several base wires twisted together. Wrap with floral tape for a final finish.

FLORAL TAPE

Floral tape does for flower fashioning what a good cosmetic does for the face. It hides a multitude of sins! It is the finishing touch for a neat, professional flower, serving to cover smoothly all the mechanics of the flower's construction. See illustration 24.

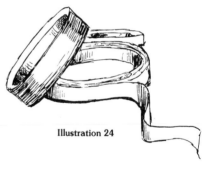

Illustration 24

Floral tape comes in a wide variety of colors, but you will most often use either light or medium green.

If you cut the floral tape in half lengthwise, you will find it useful for covering support wire.

Second, there are five essential procedures for preparing the flower: coloration, sizing, use of the pattern, wiring for support of petals and leaves, and the preparation of the stamens.

COLORATION

Very often in buying fabrics I simply buy white and then dye it. This saves shopping time. It also enables you, through the dyeing process, to provide yourself with a variety of hues. Of course, dyed fabrics do tend to fade, especially if subjected to strong light. Keep this in mind in placing your arrangement.

In dyeing, tear off a half-yard or less of fabric at a time. I use hot tap water — no need to let it boil. I put in a tablespoon of powdered dye to about a gallon of water, adding dye if I need it to get the desired color. (You may prefer the newer liquid dye. Just proportion it accordingly.)

Very often I put several pieces of fabric in the dye water at a time, taking them out two to three minutes apart. This gives each a different shade of the same color. You will be amazed at the difference you will get between the hues of a fabric you simply dip into the water and the one you let stay several minutes.

Then, you may mix dyes to produce unusual colors. Remember that the primary colors are red, blue, and yellow, but modern dye makers have mixed these with secondary colors to give you variation, from the deepest reds and purples to the fairest greens and yellows. These will often achieve your desired results, but you can go a step beyond by mixing colors. Say you want a subtle color, one not listed by the dye makers. Add a bit of this or that. To the purple dye, add a bit of blue to get a suitable iris color. To get a proper begonia, add some pink dye to orange and achieve a perfect coral.

Wetting and wringing fabrics before you dip them in the dye can give special effects. The wrinkles will take dye more readily than the remainder of the material.

Another trick is to tie-dye, tying fabric in knots before you place it in the dye. Swish it around a bit, take it out and the color is variegated. See illustration 25.

One thing is a must in dyeing: test a small piece of fabric first to see the results. Some nylon, for instance, will not absorb dye well. Try a scrap and you will know what to expect. If you are mixing colors, add a few sprinkles of the secondary one and test that too, before you proceed.

After the fabric has been dyed, roll it in an old towel to absorb excess moisture, then iron it dry.

Above all, don't be afraid of trying your hand at this dyeing business. Really, after all this explanation, it is no trick at all. Just test a piece and then have at it.

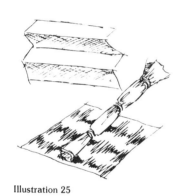

Illustration 25

SIZING

Sizing is a process through which you add body to the fabric, making it more manageable and controllable. Sizing also keeps the fabric from fraying, gives the flower you make from it more substance, and prolongs its life. Sizing is done by applying regular glue, or glue diluted with water, to the back of the fabric. Notice I said the *back* of the fabric, unless, of course, it is a fabric with no right or wrong side.

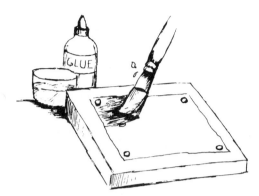

Illustration 26

To do this, cut off a piece of fabric about 12″ by 18″ and thumb-tack it to the sizing board, right side down. Brush on the glue. See illustration 26. From this point on, techniques about sizing change according to the fabric with which you are working. This is especially true with dilution of the glue.

How much glue is right for sizing? That depends on the fabric. Some fabrics are sheer. Some have a distinctive nap. Others have a tighter weave. With each you need a different procedure. It is all right for the glue to soak through the sheers, but fabrics with nap should not be saturated.

You *must* test the fabrics until you have acquired a "feel" for them so you may know the ability and reactions of each. In order to give you a running start on such testing, let me organize the sizing data by some fabric types:

Sheer fabrics—such as organdy, silk organza, voile, taffeta, lightweight cotton, dress lining material such as the silky polyesters—should be sized with regular glue thinned with water to the consistency of skimmed milk. Working with such fabrics the glue will soak through. This is fine. You simply wipe off excess with a damp cloth or paper toweling.

Once the fabric is coated, remove from the sizing board and hold the material in front of an open oven turned to 350° for a few minutes. The heat will dry the glue enough that you can put the fabric on a piece of aluminum foil to continue drying.

Velvets and satins require a different technique. Each has a distinctive surface; therefore, you do not want the glue to go through the fabric. These fabrics should be sized with a thicker solution of glue. If the backing is thick enough, just use regular glue from the jar. If not, thin it enough so that it will spread—but use less water and brush the glue onto the fabric very quickly. After the fabric has been treated, remove it from the sizing board and lay it, right side down, on aluminum foil to dry.

Velveteens and heavy cotton, such as canvas, are thicker and more closely woven. There is little danger that the glue will soak through because of the weight of the fabric and the density of its weave. This you do not want because it will disturb the surface. Use glue which is thin enough to be brushed on easily — think of painting a surface with a paint brush and latex wall paint. Do not wipe off glue. Just get the fabric well coated and lay it aside, right side down, on a piece of aluminum foil to dry.

With the sizing, I counsel experience. After just a bit of practice you will begin to develop a sense of what effect the glue will have on a particular piece of fabric.

THE PATTERN

The patterns in this book are life-sized. No enlarging or reducing is necessary. They may be traced directly from this book. In using patterns, position the tracing paper and trace the pattern, taking particular care to trace the arrow printed on the pattern. The arrow always indicates that the pattern be positioned on the material vertical with the "grain," if the material is paper. Position the pattern vertically or horizontally with the weave of fabric. Note any special directions or specifications with the patterns. Some patterns require more than one piece of fabric.

Transfer the pattern to a piece of lightweight cardboard of the type easily cut with scissors, yet heavy enough to hold its shape. This may be done by placing the tissue pattern, traced from the book, over the piece of cardboard, then with an instrument such as a ballpoint pen (with a smooth round point) bear down as you draw. This will leave the imprint on the cardboard from which you may then cut the pattern. Label fully all your cardboard patterns. Then, with the cardboard pattern as a guide, cut the fabric.

WIRING FOR SUPPORT

In working with flowers, you begin with the stem wire, a heavier wire, usually a #16 gauge. This is uncovered because it will be cloaked with floral tape as you complete the blossom. You will also be using wire as support for petals and leaves in order to give them shape and flexibility. The #22 or #24 gauge is usually needed for this purpose. The #26 gauge wire is more appropriate for long stamen stems such as lilies have. It is usually necessary that these smaller gauge wires be covered. You may cover them yourself or they can be purchased already covered with threads in green, white and other colors. They can be found in hobby shops or ordered from craft supply catalogs. Usually they come in 18" lengths. But in case you want to do your own covering, or you want another sort of colored wire, here are instructions for you to follow:

Cut ¼" strips of crepe paper cross grain, or cross-wise of the package of paper. Start with a strip of the paper about as long as the wire you plan to cover. Put some glue on the top of the wire, attach the paper and, stretching the paper, diagonally wind it down the wire. Another bit of glue at the bottom will hold the paper in its place. See illustration 27.

Wire may also be covered with the appropriate color of floral tape, such as black or brown or red, as well as green. These colors can be found in floral shops. Because of the waxy content of the floral tape, it is somewhat resistant to glue, therefore does not "hold" as quickly when glued to something. However, it is perfectly satisfactory to use as stem wire coverings. If covering a thinner gauge than #20, cut the strips of floral tape in half lengthwise, or into thirds if the wire is very thin.

After you have wrapped the wire, it is used in one of two ways as a support. It may be put between two petal pieces to hold them as you wish them to be and thus give a double petal effect; or the wire may be simply attached with glue to the back of either petal or leaf to give it support. Instructions on how to use the support with the flower parts are given with the individual directions on making each flower.

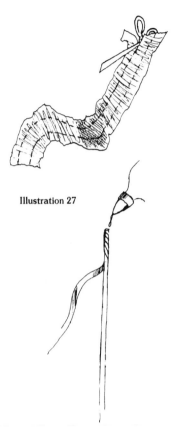

Illustration 27

THE STAMEN

The stamen is the central part of a flower. Examine a flower or a picture of a flower to determine the type of stamen. Bread dough has become one of my favorite materials for making stamens. It can be colored and shaped to almost any desired appearance.

The recipe for bread dough: 1 tablespoon of white glue to 1 slice of white bread. See illustration 28. (I usually make up three slices of bread at a time.) You may color the dough with watercolors or drops of tempera paint worked into the dough. Or, you can use the dough and color as needed afterwards with felt-tip markers or by any other method you wish. It is most important that while using the dough you keep it covered in a plastic bag, pinching out small pieces at a time. Left-over dough should be kept in a tight plastic bag stored in the refrigerator.

Stamens can be fashioned from other material — from anything which can be attached to a stem wire. You may use facial tissue with glue, absorbent

Illustration 28

cotton which has been covered or is uncovered, seeds and pods, rolled or fringed fabrics or paper, buttons and beads, ball fringe and sewing trims. If all else fails, try the pre-designed stamen in the hobby shop. See illustration 29.

Third, there are many ways to assemble the flower components into whole flowers. Each procedure is given with the individual directions on making each flower.

The final step is the measure of your artistry, an advanced procedure. It is the special attention you give to leaves and blossoms which make them into "something special."

LEAVES

Leaves, you know, are often dispensed with when working with live flowers. Take one off here and there to make your arrangement more attractive. "Tailoring" it is called by professional flower arrangers. I do not minimize the importance of leaves—even though at times I vary the leaf to improve the bouquet and often simply do not put the leaf on the flower until I am making the arrangement. The leaf is as necessary to a flower as a hairdo is to a pretty face. Usually you will want more leaves near the bottom of an arrangement to give it density. For this purpose, it is well to prepare some extras to place where you want them.

Veining is an important step in completing your flower. Veining can be done by one of two methods. You may add color to the top of the leaf, dainty color to suggest the framework of a leaf. Be careful here always to use light strokes of color to avoid a "drawn-on" look. The other method is by scoring the leaf through indenture. This you do with a small, sharp instrument. Score the leaf on its reverse side with the frame of a design. See illustration 30.

Illustration 29

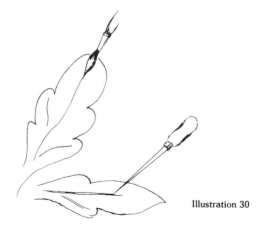

Illustration 30

32

After the leaf is veined, give it dimensions by stretching and pulling the edges, giving it this twist and that. This step provides a personality leaf instead of a flat piece of fabric.

BLOSSOMS

Blossoms appear more realistic when the edges receive attention. Stretch material for a natural shape. Roll edges for a softer appearance. Add or remove color at the rim of the blossom to give it new meaning. To add color, use a felt-tip marker, then blend the color with a watercolor brush dipped in alcohol. To subtract color, dip the brush in water to which a little household bleach has been added.

Shading colors, bleeding them to create values, can do much for your blossom. Use the felt-tip marker, then the watercolor brush dipped into the alcohol, to smooth and soften the hues. Or you may with watercolor itself, used discreetly, give new identity to your blossom. Or, you may use fabric dye in decoration. This I have tended to use more and more because it gives more varied color.

Distinctive markings, such as speckles on a day lily or the deeper colored center of a geranium, can be added with the felt-tip marker and the watercolor brush or with dye. See illustration 31. A sometimes technique for highlighting flowers is varnish. Varnish adds permanence, and it is a requirement for some flowers, such as those made from paper sacks.

Now to Flower Fashioning

Before you undertake your first flower, let me give you some tips, things I have learned over the years which might be helpful.

It is important, I think, that you make one sample flower first. This exercise affords an opportunity to get the feel of what you are doing and to make adjustments and corrections. In other words, don't spread out three yards of fabric and size it all in one confident whack. Size a small piece first. Let it dry. Then determine if it is what you want, if it has appropriate body to achieve the affect you are seeking. If not, then correct the sizing solution, either by thinning or thickening it so as to make your fabric either less stiff or stiffer. After that, follow the rest of the steps in making the sample, correcting and adjusting as necessary. This experimentation will avoid wasting materials and at the same time you will become more confident in attempting your project.

Don't be discouraged if your first effort doesn't look just dandy. Dump it in the trash and try again. Even now, you could find a "factory reject" in my

Illustration 31

wastebasket. Conversely, don't strive so much for perfection, for ready-made models. Often, a single flower can barely tolerate close inspection. Put them all in a bouquet and the charm of them becomes their almost abstract imperfection.

You might like to know how I go about my flower making. Generally, I begin with the stamen, attaching it to the main stem. Often I use bread dough for this purpose and I like it to harden overnight. Stamens are the framework for most flowers. Therefore, I make them first and set them aside. There will be, however, some occasions when it is more practical to attach the blossom itself to the stem wire, such as when the stamen consists of something like a ball fringe which is simply glued into the center of the blossom.

Next, I dye my fabrics, if necessary, and iron them dry. Then I cut them into pieces appropriate for sizing, apply the sizing, and let them dry. While these are drying, I cut patterns, label them, and organize all other materials for making the flowers. Perhaps I wrap support wire in appropriate colors and do other chores. All of the above very often will add up to one day's worth of flower making for me.

Now I have all materials ready to use and will proceed on another day to make the flowers. When convenient time arrives, I prepare petals and leaves; ripple, flute, or stretch the edges; decorate with added color; glue support wires on; or whatever my instructions call for. Finally I assemble all the parts. Often, after I have assembled the blossoms, I will go back with a watercolor brush, alcohol, and felt-tip markers, adding emphasis to the coloration and perfecting the shading effects.

There is another point to remember about your introduction to flower fashioning: don't be intimidated. Sometimes you must stand your ground. For example, you may want a flower to suit a special purpose. You decide that sheet aluminum will do the trick. You want to paint the petals red. Don't be dismayed when you go to the store and ask for red paint to coat the aluminum. The fellow may say, "Lady, you can't paint that aluminum . . . won't stay . . . got no 'tooth' in it." Go ahead and try it anyway. Maybe he was thinking about painting a barn; no cows will try your blossom. The only function of your flowers is to look pretty and the paint will surely stay put that long. Another problem is the matter of wire and the gauges which measure wire. Until you are adept at them, gauges may puzzle you. Take the measurements I have given you when you go to the store. Like as not, the salesperson, when you ask for a #22 gauge, will show you a piece and say, "Like this?" This immediately casts a doubt in your mind. Your proper answer must be something like, "Yes, like that — if that is #22 gauge. And I thank you for your help."

How-to instructions, which I am about to give you, are very much like a cooking recipe in that a long, drawn-out recipe can appear to be "too much trouble." For a fact, it can be much less complicated than it appears on first reading. Selecting the tools and materials is a major part of your effort. Putting that behind you reduces the length of your instructions. From that point on, it's just a matter of using what you have gathered together.

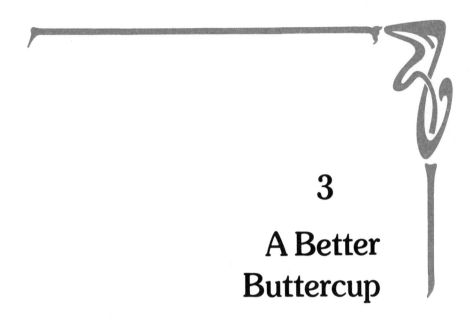

3

A Better Buttercup

Where else to start with flower fashioning than with a buttercup, that first flower which I began way back when? And what else to put with it than a daisy?

Here are two commonplace flowers, two so complementary to each other that when you join them together they become a microcosm of all the designs we use to decorate our world. Build them bold, dashing, bigger than life. No sense being miserly about these flowers. Design them into an elaborate display for your house. No need to be stingy about what you create.

I do not know what you may have called your buttercups. You may have called them ranunculas, columbine, the American cowslip. You might have called them "crowsfoot," a name distasteful to me. I think their beauty deserves better. The ones I grew up with in West Texas might have been classed botanically as evening primroses—I really do not know. We called them buttercups, five simple yellow petals brought together in a cup-shaped receptacle but so profuse they became ordinary. Seeing the golden translucent blossoms spread *en masse* beneath a mesquite tree, I often felt compelled to examine each one, comparing it with the next. Did all those little yellow powdery tendrils inside each smell the same? I discovered they made a funny noise if you knew a certain trick. Do you know how to get a buttercup to pop? Pick a nice plump bud, hold it in one hand and bring it, squash, down into the other! Perhaps it was those moments smelling and

Look bravely up into the sky,
And be content with knowing
That God wished for a buttercup
Just here, where you are growing.

JEWELL

squashing buttercups which gave me a certain reputation with my sister. I asked her recently what she recalled about the buttercups when we were children and she said, "Oh, mostly that you always came home with yellow on your nose!"

To go with a bouquet of buttercups I chose another ordinary flower, the daisy. I suppose I selected a daisy because it is an "everyday" sort of posy, not a "Sunday" one. The daisy is gay, carefree, uncluttered, naturally casual. Notice I chose a variety of paper, each golden hued, because I particularly like working with the monochromatic color scheme—shades of one color. You may prefer a fresh-as-a-daisy white.

I have made daisies out of many different materials—velvets, full-bodied cottons, even metals—but crepe paper is still my favorite material for this flower; it is also very flexible, more so than most fabrics, and more receptive to your touch. Daisies are easy to make. When they become not "fresh" after many months of use, they can be replaced with little guilt about time and money spent. At the very least, whack them across your hand and they may come out daisy-fresh.

These two, the buttercup and the daisy, are included for several reasons. If you are a novice at flower making, they provide a good opportunity to get acquainted with the art form. They are simple to construct. They are fashioned from crepe paper which is as close as your dime store. They are utility flowers, ones which work well into other designs. I have included them, too, because they are good "project" flowers which can be used if you are teaching Scouts, Y-groups, or others you may be introducing to flower fashioning.

Finally, I chose these flowers because, for all their commonplaceness, they can be fashioned into a truly distinctive arrangement. You think the buttercup and the daisy lack character? This is where your savvy, your skill, your little bit of imagination come into play. "Cup" the petals with your two thumbs and forefingers. With scissors, "curl" the leaves this way and that. Then, find your finest urn, basket, most cherished flower pot and let yourself go. Build a magnificent display of—you guessed it—buttercups and daisies.

Do be generous with them. As Diane Love said in a recently published book, *Flowers Are Fabulous*, "Flowers, like food, should be done with a lavish hand . . . . An oversized arrangement is better and more gracious than an undersized one."

Yellow Buttercup

Color Plate 1

YOU WILL NEED:

Yellow crepe paper, both single and du-plex (I use both. The translucence of the single crepe gives one effect, the opaque effect comes from the duplex.)

Orange-yellow crepe paper for stamen

Quick-sticking white glue

#20 gauge wire for stems

Needle and thread

Green floral tape

ADDITIONAL MATERIAL FOR LEAVES:

Leaf green duplex crepe paper

A memo to Flower Fashioners. Instructions for covering wire see page 31.

Step-by-step for making a buttercup

🎨 Trace and transfer patterns to cardboard and cut out. Label each.

1. MAKE THE FLOWER PARTS.

🎨 From yellow paper cut the petals.

🎨 From the green paper cut the leaves, long and loose ones, three or maybe four.

🎨 Make a small hook on one end of the #20 gauge wire cut to desired length for stems.

🎨 Using the orange-yellow crepe paper, cut a piece 2½″ by 6″ for stamen. Fold in half lengthwise but do not crease. With scissors fringe the open edge very fine to within ⅛″ of the folded edge. See illustration 1.

🎨 Spread glue along folded edge of the stamen strip. Roll as tight as possible. (I found a 4″ length of #16 gauge wire serves well to coax the small piece to roll.) See illustration 2.

🎨 Insert stem wire down through center of stamen, catching hook inside the stamen. Lay this aside to dry. See illustration 3.

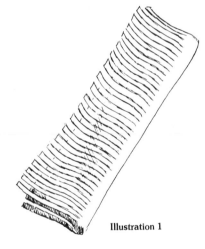

Illustration 1

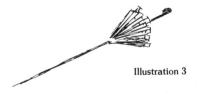

Illustration 3

Illustration 2

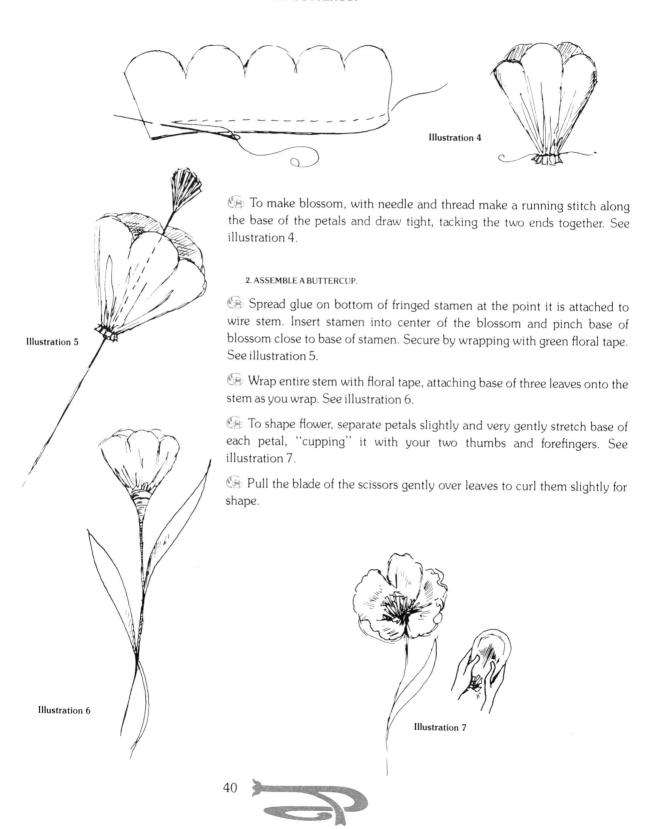

Illustration 4

Illustration 5

Illustration 6

Illustration 7

To make blossom, with needle and thread make a running stitch along the base of the petals and draw tight, tacking the two ends together. See illustration 4.

2. ASSEMBLE A BUTTERCUP.

Spread glue on bottom of fringed stamen at the point it is attached to wire stem. Insert stamen into center of the blossom and pinch base of blossom close to base of stamen. Secure by wrapping with green floral tape. See illustration 5.

Wrap entire stem with floral tape, attaching base of three leaves onto the stem as you wrap. See illustration 6.

To shape flower, separate petals slightly and very gently stretch base of each petal, "cupping" it with your two thumbs and forefingers. See illustration 7.

Pull the blade of the scissors gently over leaves to curl them slightly for shape.

Patterns for Buttercup

PETALS

⅜"

STAMEN: 2½" x 6" Rectangle fringed to within ⅛" of folded edge.

LEAF

Yellow Daisy

Color Plate 1

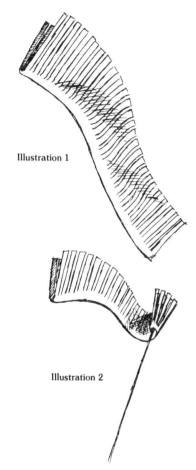

Illustration 1

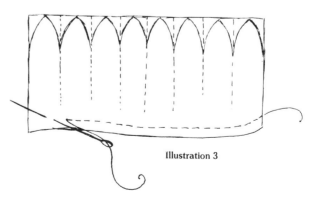

Illustration 2

YOU WILL NEED:

Yellow duplex crepe paper

Orange-yellow felt for stamen

 # 16 gauge stem wire

Quick-sticking white glue

Needle and thread

Masking tape

Green floral tape

ADDITIONAL MATERIALS FOR LEAVES:

Leaf green duplex crepe paper.

 # 22 gauge green covered wire.

Step-by-step for making a daisy:

Trace and transfer pattern to cardboard and cut out. Label.

1. MAKE THE FLOWER PARTS.

To make stamen, cut a strip of orange-yellow felt 2½″ by 12″. Fold this in half lengthwise. With scissors, finely fringe by cutting the open side to within ½″ of the folded edge. See illustration 1.

Make a small hook at one end of a piece of #16 guage stem wire cut to desired length.

Hook wire into one end of fringed strip. Spread glue along the folded edge of the fringed strip and roll around the hooked wire as tight as possible. Set aside to dry. See illustration 2.

To make petals, cut out rectangle of crepe paper 3″ by 7″. Mark off sections slightly over ⅝″ apart and cut each section down 2¼″ as indicated on the pattern. Trim and round off the petal points of each section. See illustration 3.

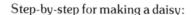

Illustration 3

42

Patterns for Daisy

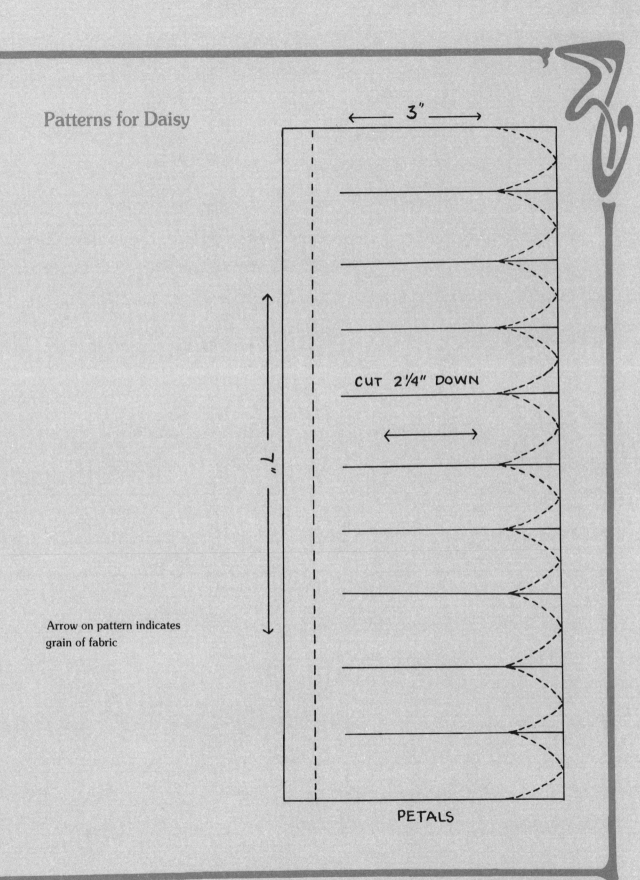

3"

"L"

CUT 2¼" DOWN

Arrow on pattern indicates
grain of fabric

PETALS

LARGE
LEAF

SMALL
LEAF

CALYX

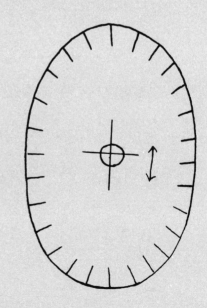

STRETCH
THIS WAY
←——→
TO MAKE
CIRCLE.

Arrow on pattern indicates grain of fabric

With needle and thread, make a running stitch $3/8''$ above the base of the petals and draw up tight. You might want to "try this on" the base of the stamen to see if it will fit and adjust accordingly. Tack the two ends together. See illustrations 3 and 4.

Place glue on the base of the stamen. Insert stamen stem into the center of the daisy petals and pull down, fixing the fringed stamen into the center of the petals. See illustration 5.

Secure the base of the petals to the wire stem with masking tape and set aside.

From the green paper, cut one calyx, two small leaves and one or more large leaves.

Cut #22 gauge covered wire into lengths, each of them 1" longer than the leaf pattern.

Gently stretch the leaves slightly to give them shape, then glue one piece of the support wire down each center back of leaf, leaving the extra inch at the base of leaf for use in attaching to the stem wire. Set aside to dry. See illustration 6.

To attach calyx, stretch the oblong-shaped calyx into a circle. Pierce a hole in the center with scissors, clip the edge of the calyx as indicated on the pattern. See illustration 7.

Coat inside of calyx with glue. Insert stem of daisy into the center hole and pull the calyx up around the base of the daisy. The glue will permit you to mold and shape it around the base of the daisy. See illustration 7.

Illustration 4

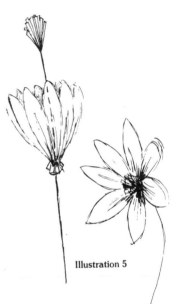

Illustration 5

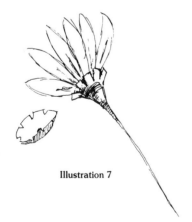

Illustration 7

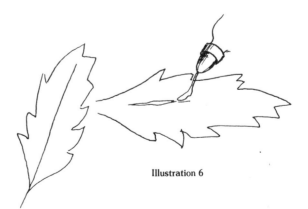

Illustration 6

2. ASSEMBLE A DAISY.

With thumb and forefingers, gently stretch each petal at the base near the center stamen. Shape and curve petals with fingers. Turn flower upside down on a cushioned surface such as a piece of foam rubber. With the point of an ice pick or similar instrument, carefully score the back of the petals three times. Ever notice how the daisy has ridges in each petal? See illustration 8.

Reshape the petals to suit you.

Wrap entire stem with floral tape, attaching two small leaves toward the top, one or more leaves down on the stem. See illustration 9.

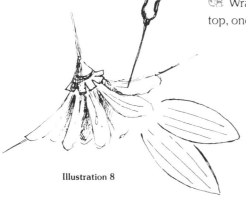

Illustration 8

Illustration 9

White Dianthus

Color Plate 1

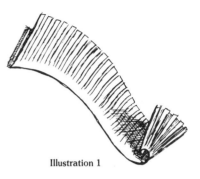

❧ Use the same pattern as for making the stamen for the buttercup, this time using white crepe paper. See illustration 1.

❧ Attach the stem wire in the same manner. Wrap with floral tape.

❧ For grassy leaves, simply cut very thin strips of crepe paper with the grain, attach to the stem with floral tape, then with blade of scissors pull along strip to curl. See illustration 2.

❧ This is a filler flower used in many a bouquet.

Illustration 1

Illustration 2

47

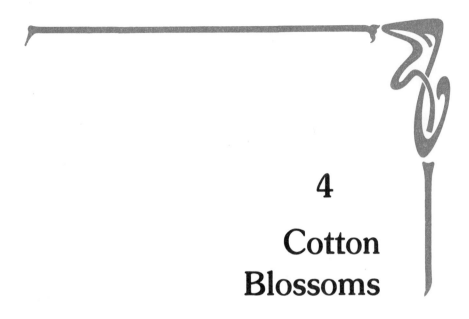

4

Cotton Blossoms

A brochure, "Flowers of Texas," published by the Texas Highway Department, declares there are more than 5,000 species of Texas wild flowers. I don't doubt it for one moment. Such handsome, roving loveliness has been emotionally stimulating to me all my life. A real treat for me is quiet, relaxing travel on some of the Texas highways at the height of wild-flower season. Drive to New Mexico in late summer, and a whole new and different crop pops up almost as if to say, "You ain't seen nothing yet." Journey even farther, up into Colorado, and as the climate becomes cooler there are still other varieties to catch your eye. "The roadside flowers," these are proudly displayed along roads and byways in all our states and provinces, too. Each patch seems to invite our attention, admiration and closer inspection. And Hawaii! There is a real haven for flower lovers!

You see, it is virtually impossible to fashion a flower that doesn't at least resemble a live one. It isn't even necessary to call it by a name. It can simply be a red flower or a yellow one or a white one. What I am saying is that if you are designing flowers for an arrangement, and the mood you want to impart requires the color turquoise, then use it. Fashion your own tastes and colors to suit your needs. You will, along the way, develop a sense of which shapes and what colors hang well with other shapes and colors.

I have chosen flowers fashioned of cotton fabrics to demonstrate this point. If you are a seamstress, there is little doubt that you are creative. There is also little doubt that you have scraps of fabric you hesitate to discard. Fashion some of these scraps into flowers. They are casual enough to be

We are the roadside flowers . . .
Lovers of idle hours,
Breakers of ordered bounds.

CARMAN

49

suitable for many occasions. They will perk up almost any room setting. Naturally, you will want to select colors carefully, harmonious with the mood you plan to create. And it may be necessary to purchase remnants, available at a great savings, to complement other scraps of fabrics you already have.

I am sure you are aware there are very few cotton fabrics available today which are entirely cotton. Most all are blends of synthetics and cotton. Actually, I am suggesting here "cotton-look" fabrics, those which have the feel and the air of cotton.

You can't make just one such posy. You will want to keep making another and another because each color and pattern creates a different feeling and an excitement in itself. These flowers are suitable for so many occasions in the life style many of us live—bridge or luncheon centerpieces, patio barbecues, birthday parties, or "just-us-folks" dinner parties. These flowers can be sophisticated or elegant or just a whimsical caricature, depending on your choice of scenes and arrangements.

I particularly like to work with shades of one color, adding just a touch of another complementary color. And I like to include opaque fabrics such as percale, and varieties of sheer cotton such as voile. The contrast creates interest in the bouquet. I am giving you here several different patterns to get you into that scrap box. I promise that when you get started you will find yourself altering the patterns and inventing ones of your own once you become familiar with the technique.

In naming these flowers I will have to give some a tag for identity, but you call them whatever you like. Winsome wild flowers? One arrangement includes a blue cotton voile poppy, a blue gingham cornflower, a blue polka-dot cornflower, a blue patterned voile columbine, a blue calico blossom, and a white cotton organdy filler flower. Then in a separate arrangement and photo, there is an eyelet and lace daisy.

Blue Cotton Voile Poppy

Color Plate 2

A memo to Flower Fashioners. Instructions for sizing, page 28. Instructions for covering wire, page 31. Bread dough recipe, page 31.

YOU WILL NEED:

Blue variegated voile, sized (I chose a variegated blue striped voile for this. The variation of color, without "hard" stripes, gives a natural effect.)

Heavy white cotton string for stamens

#22 gauge green covered wire

Quick-sticking white glue

#16 gauge wire for stems

Medium green cotton for calyx, sized

Masking tape

Green floral tape

ADDITIONAL MATERIAL FOR LEAVES:

Medium green cotton organdy, sized

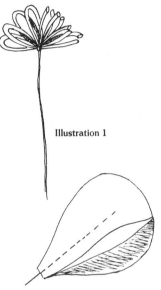

Illustration 1

Step-by-step for making a voile poppy:

🖙 Trace and transfer patterns to cardboard and cut out. Label each.

1. MAKE THE FLOWER PARTS.

🖙 To make stamens, cut a length of white string 16″ long. Fold in half three times. Twist a piece of #22 gauge wire 4″ long around the center of bundle of folded string. Clip the loops of string, making 16 stamens. See illustration 1.

🖙 Cut out 12 large petals and 10 small petals in order to put them together for six large and five small double petals.

🖙 Stretch edges of petals with your fingers to ripple slightly.

🖙 Cut six pieces of #22 gauge wire 1″ longer than large petals and five pieces 1″ longer than small petals.

🖙 To make each double petal, coat one half of wire with glue and sandwich between two petals placed back to back, leaving uncoated end of wire extended at base of petal for assembling. Allow to dry. See illustration 2.

🖙 For each blossom, cut one calyx from green cotton.

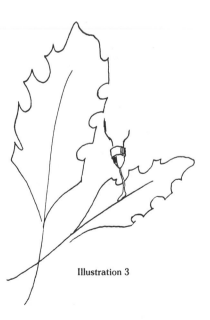

Illustration 2

2. MAKE THE LEAVES.

🖙 Cut two or three leaves for each flower from green organdy.

🖙 Cut #22 gauge green covered wire into pieces 1″ longer than leaves. With quick-sticking glue, attach wire to center back of leaf, leaving about 1½″ extended at base for attaching to stem. Allow to dry. See illustration 3.

Illustration 3

3. ASSEMBLE THE VOILE POPPY.

Arrange five small double petals around center stamens of string. Then arrange six large double petals around the five small ones. Twist all extended wire ends together. See illustration 4.

Place desired length of #16 gauge wire alongside the twisted petal stems and secure with masking tape. See illustration 4.

Punch a hole in center of calyx and insert stem of flower. Place glue on inside of calyx, bring up around base of blossom and attach.

Wrap entire stem of wire with floral tape, attaching leaves as you wrap. See illustration 5.

Illustration 4

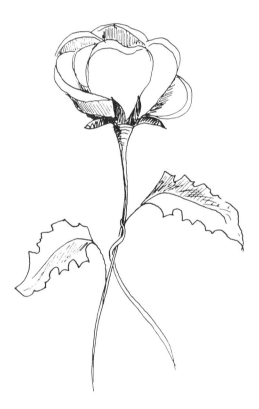

Illustration 5

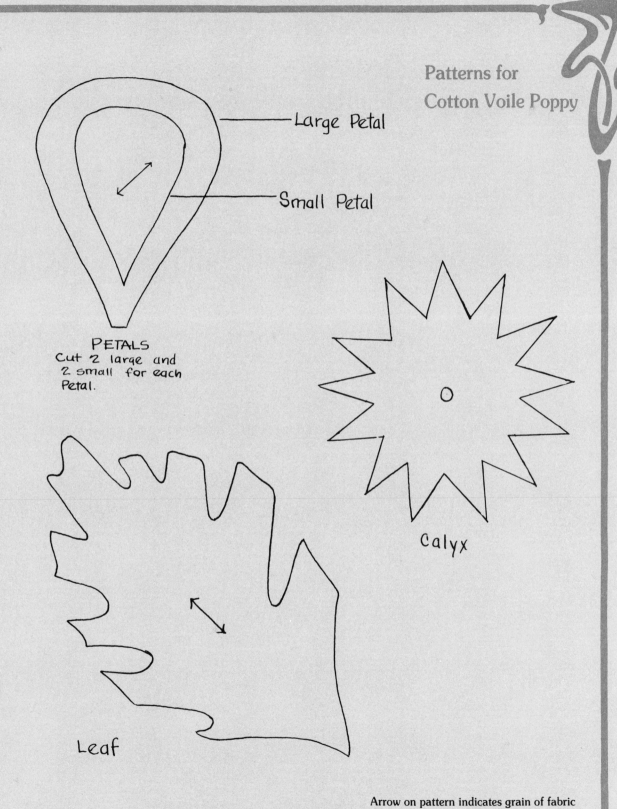

Patterns for
Cotton Voile Poppy

Large Petal

Small Petal

PETALS
Cut 2 large and
2 small for each
Petal.

Calyx

Leaf

Arrow on pattern indicates grain of fabric

Blue Gingham Cornflower

Color Plate 2

YOU WILL NEED:

Blue-checked cotton gingham (I used gingham in two shades of blue rather than blue and white.)

Spray starch

Quick-sticking white glue

#16 gauge stem wire

Green floral tape

ADDITIONAL MATERIALS
FOR LEAVES AND CALYXES:

Medium green cotton fabric for calyxes, sized

Medium green cotton organdy for leaves, sized

#22 gauge green covered wire

Step-by-step for making cornflower:

Trace and transfer patterns to cardboard and cut out. Label each.

1. MAKE THE FLOWER PARTS.

Heavily spray starch gingham fabric and iron.

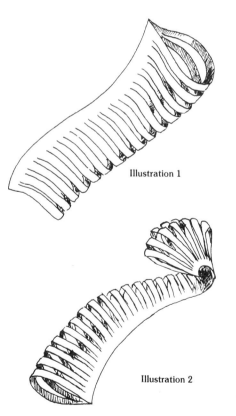

Illustration 1

Illustration 2

For each blossom, cut a piece of gingham 3″ by 12″. Fold in half lengthwise but do not crease. Glue open edges together. With scissors fringe in ¹/₁₆″ slits the folded edge to within ½″ of glued edge. See illustration 1.

Place glue on unfringed edge, then roll as tight as possible. See illustration 2.

Make a small hook at one end of #16 gauge stem wire. Insert into center of blossom. Pull down, catching hook on fabric inside blossom. See illustration 3.

Cut calyx from green cotton fabric. Clip edge according to instructions on pattern.

Place glue on base of blossom. Wrap calyx around base of blossom. See illustration 4.

2. MAKE THE LEAVES.

Cut from green organdy two small and one or more large leaves for each blossom.

Cut #22 gauge green covered wire into pieces 1″ longer than leaf pattern.

✆ With quick-sticking glue, attach wire to center back of leaf, leaving about 1½″ extended at base for attaching to stem. Allow to dry. See illustration 5.

3. ASSEMBLE THE CORNFLOWER.

✆ Wrap entire stem, beginning at calyx, attaching two small leaves near top and one or more larger leaves further down on stem. See illustration 6.

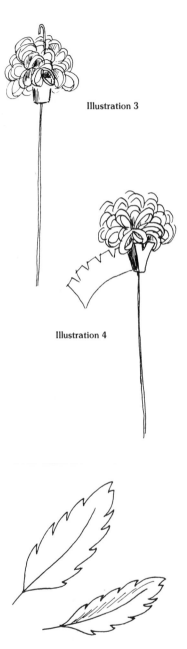

Illustration 3

Illustration 4

Illustration 6

Blue Polka-Dot Cotton Cornflower

Color Plate 2

Illustration 5

Instructions for making this flower are the same as those for the gingham cornflower except that in order to make a larger blossom, fabric should be cut in pieces 4¼″ by 12½″ and calyx pattern is larger to conform to large flowers. Leaves may be made the same as gingham cornflower leaves.

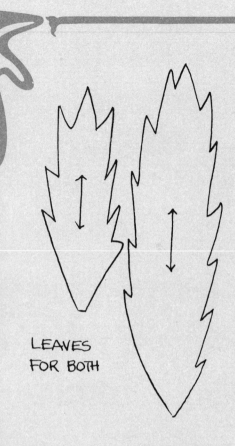

Patterns for Gingham Cornflower

PETALS ARE
3" X 12"
RECTANGLE

LEAVES
FOR BOTH

CALYX

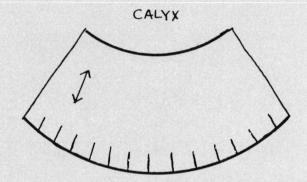

Arrow on pattern indicates grain of fabric

Patterns for Polka-Dot Cornflower

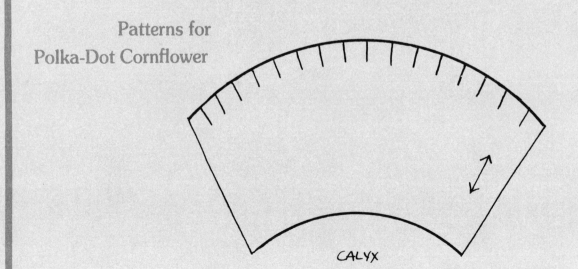

CALYX

Blue-Patterned Voile Columbine

Color Plate 2

YOU WILL NEED:

Blue-patterned cotton voile, sized

Quick-sticking white glue

Bread dough for stamens (See recipe, page 31.)

 # 22 gauge green covered wire

Masking tape

Green floral tape

 # 16 gauge wire for stem

ADDITIONAL MATERIAL FOR LEAVES:

Medium green cotton organdy, sized

Step-by-step for making voile columbine:

🌸 Trace and transfer patterns to cardboard and cut out. Label them.

1. MAKE THE FLOWER PARTS.

🌸 To make stamens, cut five pieces of #22 gauge green covered wire 3″ long. Glue a small pea-sized piece of bread dough, flattened slightly, on end of each wire. Set aside to dry thoroughly. See illustration 1.

Illustration 1

🌸 For each blossom, cut five petals and five pieces of #22 gauge wire 1″ longer than petals. Stretch edges of petals with fingers to ripple them slightly.

🌸 With quick-sticking glue, attach a length of green covered wire to the center back of each petal, leaving about 1½″ extended at base for assembling. Allow to dry. See illustration 2.

2. MAKE THE LEAVES.

🌸 From green organdy, cut two or more leaves for each blossom.

🌸 Cut #22 gauge green covered wire into pieces 1″ longer than leaf pattern.

Illustration 2

🌸 With quick-sticking glue, attach wire to center back of leaf, leaving about 1½″ extended at base for attaching to stem. Allow to dry. See Voile Poppy Illustration 3, page 51.

3. ASSEMBLE THE VOILE COLUMBINE.

Twist together five stamens for center of flower.

Place five petals, evenly spaced, around center. Twist all wires together. See illustration 3.

Place desired length of #16 gauge wire alongside the twisted petal stems and secure with masking tape.

Wrap entire stem with floral tape, attaching two or three leaves along stem as you wrap. See illustration 4.

Shape petals.

Illustration 3

Illustration 4

Patterns for Calico Blossom

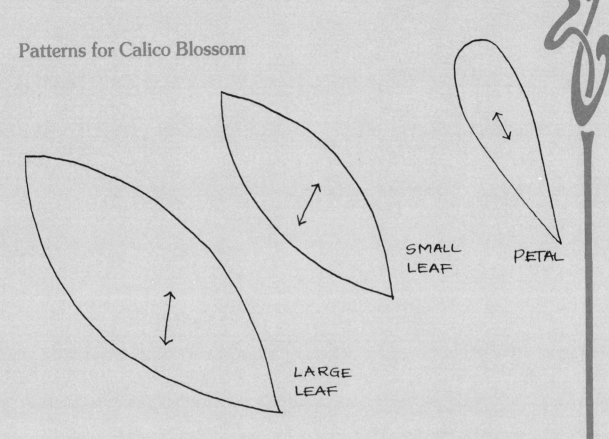

SMALL
LEAF

PETAL

LARGE
LEAF

Arrow on pattern indicates grain of fabric

Patterns for Voile Columbine

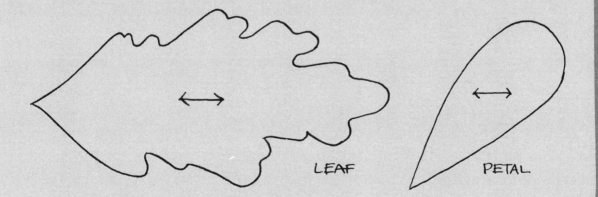

LEAF

PETAL

Blue Calico Blossom

Color Plate 2

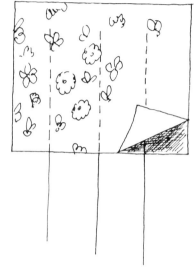

YOU WILL NEED:

Blue-patterned cotton calico

Fusible webbing (A translucent web of fibers that fuse with the heat of an iron to join two layers of fabric together.)

Red-orange pom-pons cut from ball fringe

Quick-sticking white glue

 # 22 gauge green covered wire

 # 16 gauge stem wire

Masking tape

Green floral tape

ADDITIONAL MATERIAL FOR LEAVES:

Medium green cotton organdy, sized

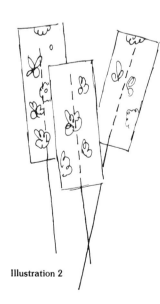

Illustration 1

Step-by-step for making a calico blossom:

Trace and transfer patterns to cardboard and cut out. Label them.

1. MAKE THE FLOWER PETALS.

For each blossom, you will need 15 petals. To make three petals at a time, cut a 3½″ square double layer of calico and a single thickness of fusible webbing the same size.

Place the fusible webbing and three 4½″ wires spread evenly apart between the calico layers, leaving about half of the wire extended below fabric square. See illustration 1.

Fuse fabrics together according to package instructions.

Cut into three pieces, each with a wire in between. See illustration 2.

Make five of these squares of three petals for each flower.

Center petal pattern on each wired piece and cut around the pattern to make petals. See illustration 3.

2. MAKE THE LEAVES.

From green organdy, cut two small and one or more large leaves for each blossom.

Cut #22 gauge green covered wire into pieces 1″ longer than leaf pattern.

Illustration 2

🌸 With quick-sticking glue, attach wire to center back of leaf, leaving about 1½″ extended at base for attaching to stem. Allow to dry. See illustration 4.

3. ASSEMBLE THE CALICO BLOSSOM.

🌸 Twist together the extended base wires of 15 petals. You might rather use pliers to do this.

🌸 Shape petals, then glue a red-orange pom-pon in center.

🌸 Place a desired length of #16 gauge stem wire alongside the twisted blossom wire and secure with masking tape.

🌸 Wrap entire stem with floral tape, attaching two small leaves near top of stem, then one or more larger leaves below. See illustration 5.

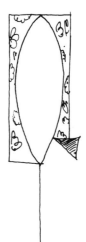

Illustration 3

Illustration 5

Illustration 4

White Cotton Organdy Filler Flower

Color Plate 2

Illustration 1

Illustration 2

Illustration 3

YOU WILL NEED:

White organdy
 # 28 fine gauge green covered wire
 # 20 gauge wire for stem

Dark green crepe paper for leaves
Masking tape
Green floral tape

Step-by-step for filler flower:

Trace pattern, transfer to cardboard and cut out. Label each.

1. MAKE THE FLOWER PARTS.

Cut three petals for each flower.

Cut a length of # 28 gauge wire 3″ long.

Twist center of wire around center of petal, twisting petals also. Now separate the two strands of wire and twist around second petal. Again, separate the wire and twist around third petal. When completed, this should give the appearance of six petals. See illustrations 1, 2, and 3.

2. ASSEMBLE THE FILLER FLOWER.

Lay twisted wire ends alongside a length of # 20 gauge stem wire. Secure the twisted wire with a tiny strip of masking tape.

Wrap entire stem with floral tape, attaching two or three very thin strips of green crepe paper about 6″ long. Pull blade of scissors over strips of crepe paper to curl them. See illustration 4.

Illustration 4

Patterns for Filler Flower

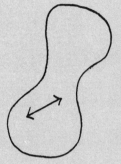

PETAL

Cut 3 For Each Petal

Pattern for Leaves/Eyelet and Lace Daisies

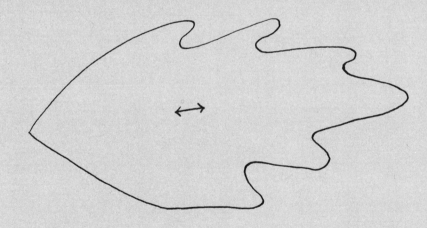

POLKA DOT LEAF
FOR EYELET

SOLID LEAF
FOR LACE

Arrow on pattern indicates grain of fabric

The Eyelet Daisy

Color Plate 3 (As seen in Family Circle Magazine*)*

Illustration 1

Illustration 2

YOU WILL NEED:

2″ wide eyelet ruffle, 9″ for each flower

Spray starch

Green pom-pons cut from ball fringe

Quick-sticking white glue

Needle and thread

 # 16 gauge stem wire

Green floral tape

ADDITIONAL MATERIALS FOR LEAVES:

Green and white polka-dot percale

Fusible webbing (A translucent web of fibers that fuse with the heat of an iron to join two layers of fabric together.)

 # 22 gauge green covered wire

Step-by-step for making daisy:

1. MAKE THE FLOWER PARTS.

Prepare stem by gluing green pom-pon to end of #16 gauge stem wire and allow to dry. See illustration 1.

Cut a 9″ length of 2″ white eyelet ruffle.

Glue ends together, forming a circle and allow to dry.

With needle and thread, make a running stitch around base of ruffle circle. Gather up as tight as possible and tack thread. See illustration 2.

Put glue on base of pom-pon on stem wire. Insert stemmed pom-pon into center of eyelet circle, fixing the pom-pon in center to serve as a stamen. See illustration 3.

Spray eyelet lightly with starch and allow to dry.

2. MAKE THE LEAVES.

Cut # 22 gauge covered wire into 6″ lengths.

Trace and transfer patterns to cardboard and cut out. Label each.

For each leaf, cut two pieces of green polka-dot fabric and one piece of fusible web 2½″ by 4½″. Lay the two pieces of fabric back to back together with fusible web between.

Place a 6″ piece of wire in center of square between fabrics, leaving about 2″ extended beyond base. See illustration 4. Press all together according to manufacturer's instructions.

Illustration 3

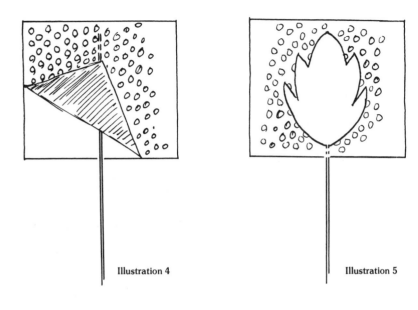

Illustration 4

Illustration 5

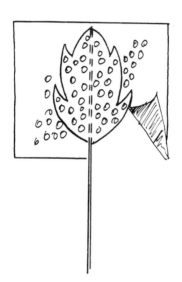

Illustration 6

🖐 Position leaf pattern on bonded fabric piece so that wire is in center of pattern. Draw around pattern and then cut out leaf. See illustrations 5 and 6.

3. ASSEMBLE THE DAISY.

🖐 Wrap entire stem of daisy with floral tape, attaching two or three leaves as you wrap. See illustration 7.

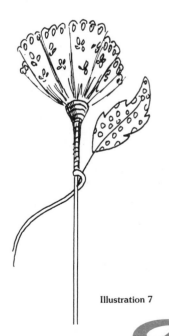

Illustration 7

65

The Lace Daisy

Color Plate 3 (As seen in Family Circle Magazine)

YOU WILL NEED:

1" wide scalloped lace trim, 5 scallops for each flower

Small, round, green buttons with two eyes on back (If you can't find these, buy white ones and color with a green felt-tip marker.)

Needle and thread

 # 22 gauge green covered wire

Quick-sticking white glue

Green floral tape

ADDITIONAL MATERIALS FOR LEAVES:

Solid green percale

Fusible webbing (A translucent web of fibers that fuse with the heat of an iron to join two layers of fabric together.)

Step-by-step for making lace daisy:

1. MAKE THE FLOWER PARTS.

🌸 Insert one end of #22 gauge stem wire, cut to desired length, through the holes in the button shank. Twist end tightly with pliers. See illustration 1.

🌸 Cut and gather the lace as directed for eyelet daisy, using five or perhaps six scallops of lace depending on their width. See illustration 2.

🌸 Insert stemmed button into lace circle and glue gathered edge to base of button.

Illustration 1

2. MAKE THE LEAVES.

🌸 Cut #22 gauge wire into 6" lengths.

🌸 Trace pattern and transfer to cardboard and cut out. Label it.

🌸 For four leaves, cut a 4" square double layer of green fabric and a single thickness of fusible webbing the same size.

Illustration 2

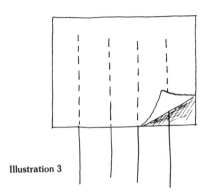

Illustration 3

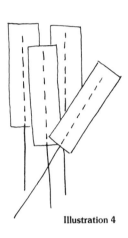

Illustration 4

🌸 Place the webbing and four 6" stem wires, 1" apart, between the fabric layers leaving about 2" of wire extended. See illustration 3.

🌸 Press together according to package instructions.

🌸 Cut into four pieces, each with a wire in center. See illustration 4.

🌸 Position leaf pattern on each piece of bonded fabric so that wire is in center of pattern. Draw around pattern and then cut out leaf. See illustration 5.

3. ASSEMBLE THE LACE DAISY.

🌸 Wrap entire stem of flower with floral tape, attaching two or three leaves as you wrap. See illustration 6.

Illustration 5

Illustration 6

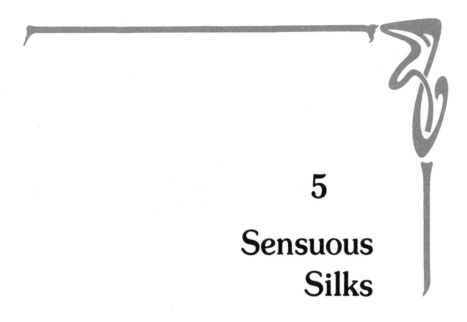

5

Sensuous
Silks

Would you like to make a flower people would instinctively smell to see if it were real? Try the silk blossoms, the so-called "sensuous flowers," those which imply delight in color, form, and suggested aroma.

These flowers are like the pleasures of the world.

SCOTT

When people refer now to "silk flowers" they are usually referring to one of these—but understand that "real" silk is rarely real. Oh, you can find it. It is sometimes put into roses or other coveted flowers, many of which are very old. These pure silks are usually imported and very costly. And though they make lovely flowers, frankly I do not think they have the practical quality which is desired in flower fashioning. Try some if you wish, but you may have better luck if you stick to those fabrics which have the feel of silk, the soft aspects: rayons, acetates, taffetas, satins, cottons, sheers. Really, when people speak of silk flowers they are often speaking about those which are neither plastic, paper or metal—fabric flowers, as it were. Such flowers have the fragile appearance which is lifelike. They make you want to feel or smell the beauty. Perhaps you will someday devise a way to give your fashioned flowers a fragrance. Not a bad idea!

It is such a task, selecting from the wide variety of silklike fabrics those which are included in this book. There are opaques and sheers. A mixture of fabrics and techniques can make an unusually lovely arrangement. Certainly I enthusiastically encourage you to try these and to invent other patterns and techniques of your own. After such experimenting, I can imagine you will find yourself in a fabric store visually fashioning blossoms out of every bolt you see.

The flowers I selected for one arrangement are mostly bulb-type flowers, the first to appear in the spring, most of them made of taffeta with one technique. Is it because they are so welcome, after a cold blossomless winter, that they are unusually beautiful when they show their faces? Or are bulb flowers just unique? Whatever, they come just as our souls are needing them. The crocus, the daffodil, the tulip, and the iris . . . I read the other day that the iris comes to us in a wider range of colors than any other flower.

The iris, tulip, and day lily in the arrangement were originally made for and seen in *Family Circle Magazine*. I am combining them here in Color Plate 4 with other spring flowers. The tulips, iris, and daffodils require the use of a hot iron in making. Two pieces of fabric are glued together by a center wire covered with quick-sticking glue. The fabric is then just barely touched with the iron—a quick, down-and-up motion. The pieces will separate slightly and the taffeta will crinkle and ruffle to create interesting effects and to add dimension. While this is a simple, easy technique, different fabric contents will respond in different ways. It is *vital*, therefore, to experiment with *your iron* and *your* fabric to determine how much heat is required.

With the iris—which must surely be one of my favorite flowers—I selected two like examples, one a creamy off-white with yellow "beards," the other in shades of lavender with purple marking its throat. For purposes of instruction, I will give you fabric for only the purple. Choose whatever color you wish because, no doubt, there is a color of iris similar.

Once as I was dyeing fabrics, preparing to make flowers, the most marvelous special effect happened. Fabric dye instructions will tell you to wet the fabric before immersing in the dye bath. I did this, and in so doing I wadded the material. Before I could get it smoothed, I found the wrinkles had taken the dye first. These simulated the most realistic veins! From that point, I would purposely wrinkle the fabric to achieve the effect, giving the iris very delicate, tracerylike veins. Unfortunately, this is not evident to you in the photograph, but do try it.

The flowers for the other arrangement are the poppies, the single most popular flower I make. When first I began this book, friends said to me, "I hope you plan to include some silk poppies." And so I did. The poppies offer a quick explosion of color to an otherwise drab room. They are quite happy arranged by themselves and they take little experience arranging. They are attractive in a dramatic line arrangement or very pleasing just plopped into an old churn, pewter pitcher, or black iron pot. If you chance to use them massed, plan on making plenty of leaves and several buds.

Do experiment, please, with your choice of fabrics. Using this technique, with no support wire in the petals, be sure to select a fabric which will adapt well to the process of sizing and pleating. I chose a semitransparent piece of silky looking synthetic blend. A thin solution of water and glue brushed onto the fabric gave it just the right amount of body for the petals to pleat well and stand on their own. If your fabric is softer and doesn't react as well, try cutting the size of the petals down to make a smaller flower. Other fabrics which will adapt well to this pattern and technique are organdy and some full-bodied taffetas. I like to make them of fabrics which are translucent, if not transparent. Quite often I like to mix hot pinks, reds, and oranges.

The Tulip

Color Plate 4

YOU WILL NEED:

Orange taffeta (I suggest using two or three different shades. Dye if necessary.)

Orange, red, and yellow felt-tip markers

Small watercolor brush

Rubbing alcohol

Quick-sticking white glue

Bread dough for stamens (See recipe, page 31.)

#22 gauge covered wire, white and green

#16 gauge wire for stem

Masking tape

Green floral tape

ADDITIONAL MATERIALS FOR LEAVES:

2¾" wide green floral ribbon

Green felt-tip marker

Regular glue

A memo to Flower Fashioners Instructions for covering wire, page 31. Bread dough recipe, page 31

Illustration 1

Step-by-step for making the tulip:

Trace and transfer patterns to cardboard and cut out. Label them.

1. MAKE THE FLOWER PARTS.

To make three stamens for each blossom, cut three 5" lengths of green covered #22 wire.

Glue a bit of bread dough about the size of a pea at one end of the stem, rolling between fingers to shape. Color with yellow felt-tip marker. See illustration 1.

For each flower, cut 12 petals from taffeta. This makes six double petals.

Lightly touch the edges with orange or red felt-tip marker. With watercolor brush dipped in alcohol, touch edges to make colors bleed. See illustration 2.

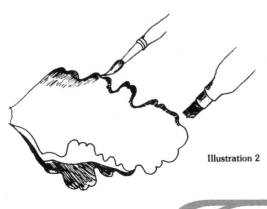

Illustration 2

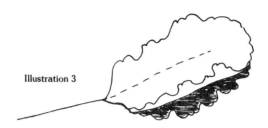

Illustration 3

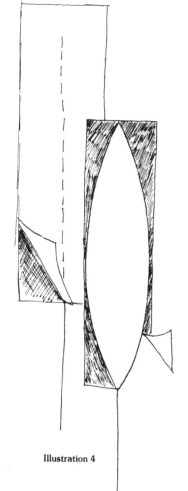

Illustration 4

🎨 Cut #22 gauge white covered wire into six 5″ lengths.

🎨 Coat about 3½″ of each wire with quick-sticking glue. Sandwich between two petals, leaving uncoated end of wire extended at base for assembling. Let dry completely. See illustration 3.

🎨 With a very hot iron, touch each double petal with a very quick down-and-up motion. Be sure to test this step on scraps first.

2. MAKE THE LEAVES.

🎨 For each leaf, cut two 7″ pieces of green floral ribbon.

🎨 Cut #22 gauge green covered wire into 9″ lengths.

🎨 Coat wrong side of one ribbon with regular glue.

🎨 Sandwich the two ribbons together, back to back, with wire between, leaving 2″ extended at one end for attaching to stem. Allow to dry. See illustration 4.

🎨 Center leaf pattern on wired ribbon and cut out shape. See illustration 4.

🎨 With a green felt-tip marker, very lightly stroke the leaf from base toward the stem to simulate veins. See illustration 5.

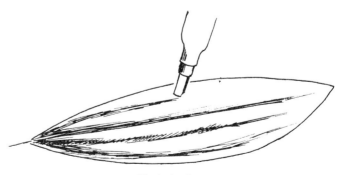

Illustration 5

3. ASSEMBLE THE TULIP.

✿ Place three stamens in the center of six petals.

✿ Twist all extended wires from the stamens and the six petals together. See illustration 6.

✿ Lay a desired length of #16 gauge wire alongside the twisted petals and stamens and secure with masking tape. See illustration 7.

✿ Wrap entire stem with floral tape, attaching two leaves for each blossom, placing them rather low on the stem. See illustration 8.

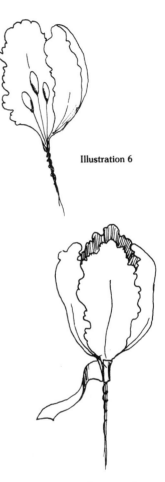

Illustration 6

Illustration 7

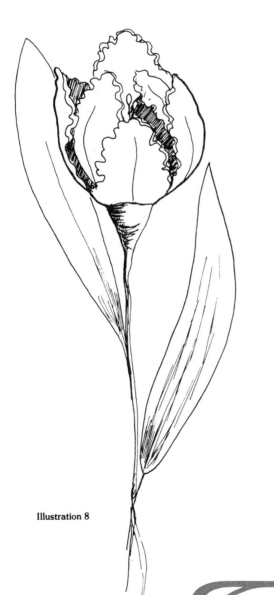

Illustration 8

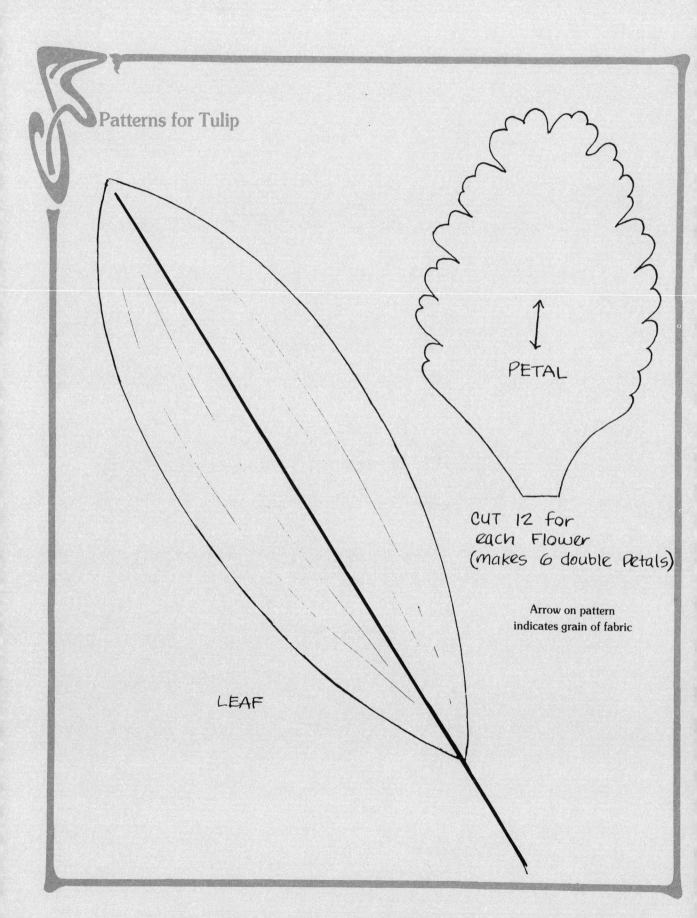

Patterns for Tulip

PETAL

CUT 12 for
each Flower
(makes 6 double Petals)

Arrow on pattern
indicates grain of fabric

LEAF

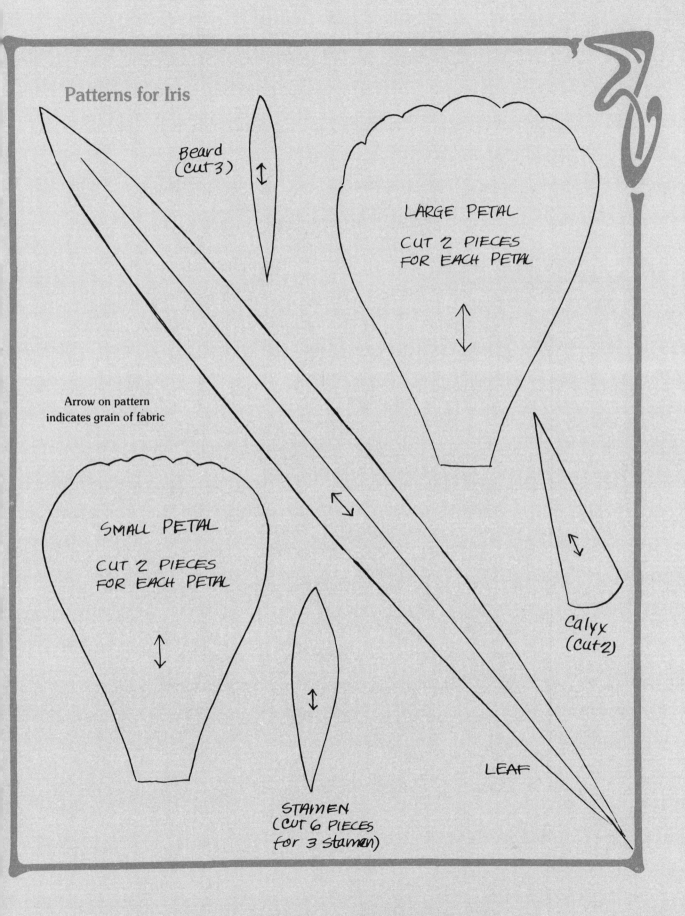

Patterns for Iris

Beard
(Cut 3)

LARGE PETAL

CUT 2 PIECES
FOR EACH PETAL

Arrow on pattern
indicates grain of fabric

SMALL PETAL

CUT 2 PIECES
FOR EACH PETAL

Calyx
(Cut 2)

LEAF

STAMEN
(CUT 6 PIECES
for 3 stamen)

The Iris

Color Plate 4

YOU WILL NEED:

Taffeta, dyed shades of purple (I used a very fine, tightly woven grade of taffeta and about one tablespoon of purple dye in a half-gallon of hot tap water with just a sprinkling of blue dye. Test the color on a scrap, then add more blue if needed.)

Purple felt-tip marker

Small watercolor brush

Rubbing alcohol

 # 22 gauge white covered wire

 # 16 gauge stem wire

Scraps of yellow crushed velvet or velvet ribbon for "beard"

Quick-sticking white glue

Masking tape

Green floral tape

ADDITIONAL MATERIALS FOR LEAVES:

1½" spring-green satin floral ribbon

Regular glue

 # 22 gauge green covered wire

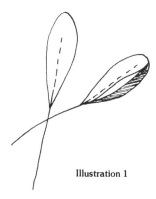

Illustration 1

Illustration 2

Step-by-step for making the iris:

Trace and transfer patterns to cardboard and cut out. Label them.

1. MAKE THE FLOWER PARTS.

For stamens, cut six pieces of taffeta from pattern to make three double stamens and cut three 4" pieces of # 22 wire.

Coat 2" of the wire with glue and sandwich between stamen petals, leaving the other 2" extended. Let dry. Color darker purple with purple felt-tip marker. See illustration 1.

From yellow velvet scraps, cut three "beard" patterns.

From taffeta cut six large petals and six small petals to make three large double and three small double petals.

Very lightly touch petal edges with purple felt-tip marker. With watercolor brush dipped in alcohol, touch edges, bleeding the colors. Also make markings around base of petal and soften with alcohol. See illustration 2.

Cut # 22 gauge white covered wire into 5" lengths. Coat 3" with glue. Sandwich the wire, centered, between each pair of petals with uncoated wire extended at base. You now have six double petals. See illustration 3.

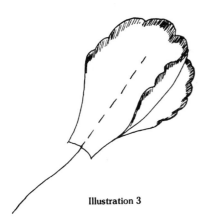

Illustration 3

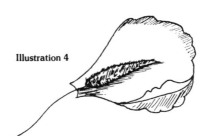

Illustration 4

With a very hot iron, touch each double petal with a quick, down-and-up motion. You may want to do this on both sides. Test the technique on scraps first.

Glue the yellow "beard" to the three large petals, starting at the base, gluing upwards. See illustration 4.

2. MAKE THE LEAVES.

For each leaf, cut two 10″ pieces of spring-green floral ribbon and one 12″ piece of #22 gauge green covered wire. See Tulip Illustration 4, page 74.

Coat wrong side of one ribbon with regular glue.

Center the wire on the glue and sandwich the two ribbons together, back to back, with wire between, leaving 2″ extended at one end for attaching to stem. Allow to dry.

Center leaf pattern on wired ribbon and cut out shape.

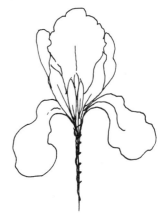

Illustration 5

3. ASSEMBLE THE IRIS.

Place the three stamens in the center of the petals with the three small petals on the inside, the larger petals on the outside. Twist all stems together. See illustration 5.

Cut two calyx pieces out of floral ribbon and glue to base of flower petals, points upward. See illustration 6.

Illustration 6

Cut # 16 gauge stem wire to desired lengths, lay alongside twisted petal stems and secure with masking tape.

Wrap entire stem with floral tape, attaching leaves, two for each flower, placed rather low on the stem.

To shape the iris, cup the three center petals toward the stamens, bend the three outside petals downward. See illustration 7.

Illustration 7

COLOR PLATE 1

A Better Buttercup plus
Daisies and Dianthus

*Instructions for buttercup, page
39; daisy, page 42; dianthus, page 47.*

COLOR PLATE 2

Cotton Blossoms

Instructions for blue cotton voile poppy, page 51; blue gingham cornflower, page 54; blue polka-dot cotton cornflower, page 55; blue-patterned voile columbine, page 57; blue calico blossoms, page 60; white organdy filler flower, page 62.

ARRANGED BY CHARLOTTE QUACKENBUSH

COLOR PLATE 3

Daisies

Instructions for eyelet daisy, page 64; lace daisy, page 66.

AS SEEN IN **FAMILY CIRCLE**

ARRANGED BY CHARLOTTE QUACKENBUSH

Sensuous Silks

Instructions for the tulip, page 73; the iris, page 78; the day lily, page 89; daffodil, page 93; johnny jump-up, page 95.

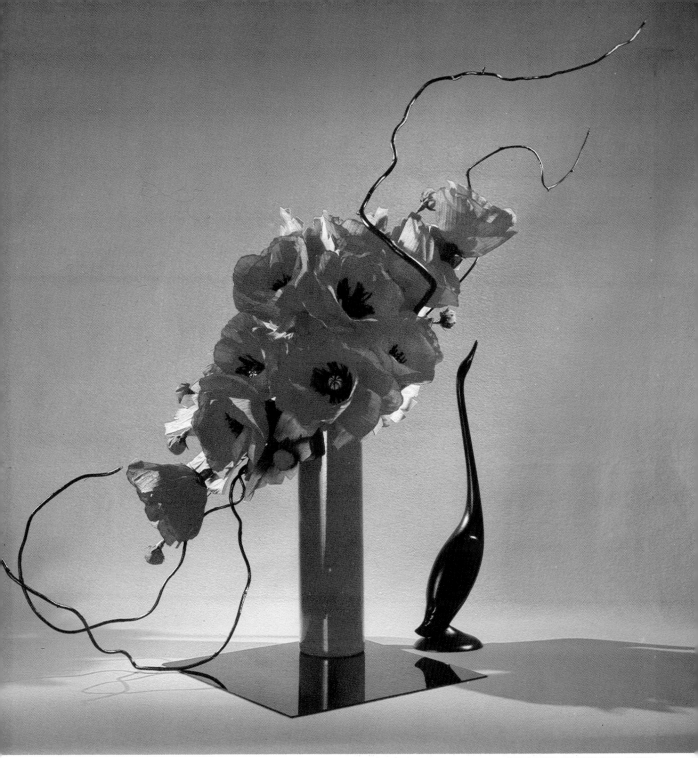

COLOR PLATE 5

Blazing Poppies

Instructions for poppy, page 98.

COLOR PLATE 6 **The Yellow Rose of Texas** *Instructions for organdy rose, page 108.*

COLOR PLATE 7

White Silk Lily

Instructions for silk lily, page 112.

ARRANGED BY DUSTY McGUIRE

(overleaf)
COLOR PLATE 8

Velvet Tulip

Instructions for the tulip,
page 123.

AS SEEN IN **FAMILY CIRCLE**

Day Lilies

Color Plate 4

YOU WILL NEED:

Pale yellow taffeta, sized

Bread dough (See recipe, page 31.)

Yellow and orange felt-tip markers

Small watercolor brush

Rubbing alcohol

Quick-sticking white glue

#26 gauge green covered wire for stamens

#24 gauge white covered wire

#16 gauge stem wire

Masking tape

Green floral tape

ADDITIONAL MATERIALS FOR LEAVES:

Chartreuse satin floral ribbon, 3" wide

Regular glue

#22 gauge green covered wire

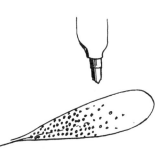

Illustration 1

Step-by-step for making a day lily:

Trace and transfer patterns to cardboard and cut out. Label each.

1. MAKE THE FLOWER PARTS.

Make six stamens for each flower. Cut #26 gauge green covered wire into 5" lengths. At the end of each wire, glue a pea-sized piece of dough, rolling it between fingers to form a thin stamen about ½" long. See illustration 1. Flatten slightly. Dry overnight, then color stamens with either yellow or orange felt-tip marker.

Cut out of taffeta 12 petals for each flower. This will make six double petals.

For petals cut #24 gauge white covered wire into six 5" lengths.

Coat 3" of each length with quick-sticking glue and sandwich, centered, between two petals leaving uncoated end at base for assembly. Allow to dry. See illustration 2.

Using yellow and orange felt-tip markers, dot the petals near the center base. See illustration 3. With watercolor brush dipped into alcohol, touch dots, bleeding and softening the colors.

Illustration 2

Illustration 3

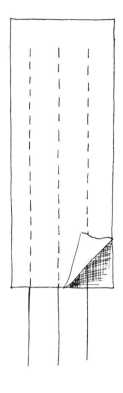

Illustration 4

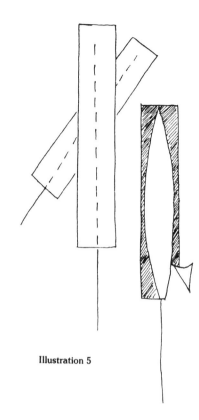

Illustration 5

Illustration 6

2. MAKE THE LEAVES.

⟐ Cut three 11″ lengths of #22 gauge green covered wire.

⟐ Cut two 9″ lengths of chartreuse floral ribbon, 3″ wide.

⟐ Coat wrong side of one ribbon with regular glue.

⟐ Place the three wires on the glue, spacing 1″ apart, leaving 2″ extended below base for assembly. See illustration 4.

⟐ Place the other ribbon on top, sandwiching the two ribbons, back to back, with the wires in between. Allow to dry. See illustration 4.

⟐ Cut the three wires apart. Center leaf pattern on each wired part and cut out the leaf shape. See illustration 5.

3. ASSEMBLE THE DAY LILY.

⟐ Place the extended base wires of the six double petals around the six stamens and twist wires together. See illustration 6.

90

🌀 Cut #16 gauge stem wire to desired lengths. Lay alongside twisted petals and secure with masking tape.

🌀 Wrap entire stem with green floral tape, attaching leaves as you wrap.

🌀 Shape petals into lily forms. See illustration 7.

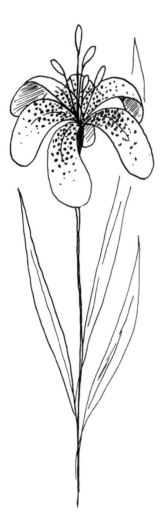

Illustration 7

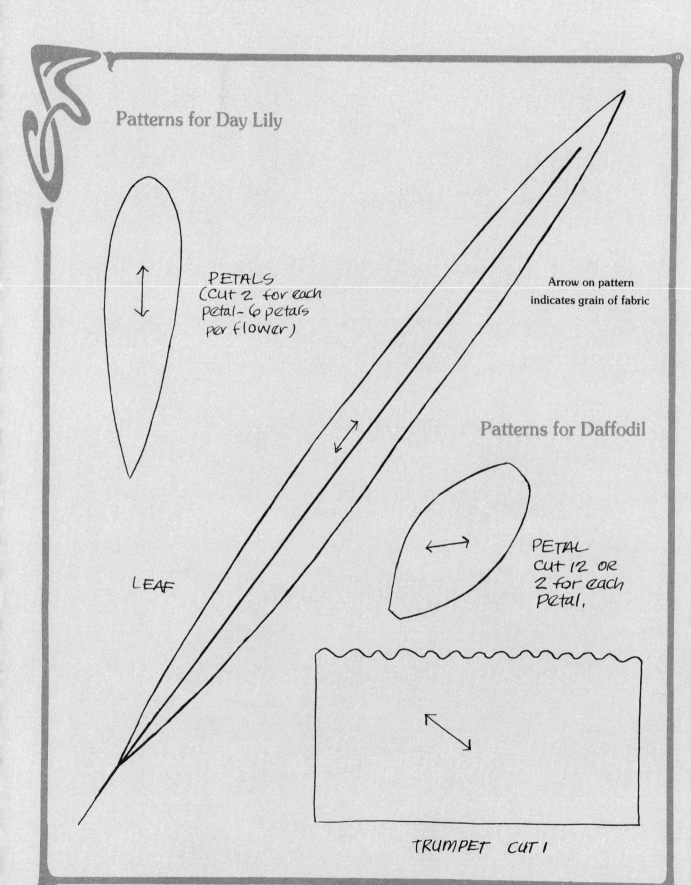

Patterns for Day Lily

PETALS
(Cut 2 for each
petal- 6 petals
per flower)

Arrow on pattern
indicates grain of fabric

Patterns for Daffodil

LEAF

PETAL
Cut 12 OR
2 for each
Petal.

TRUMPET CUT 1

Yellow Daffodils

Color Plate 4

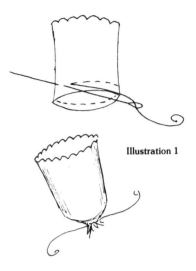

Illustration 1

YOU WILL NEED:

Yellow taffeta, sized
Orange felt-tip marker
Quick-sticking white glue
Needle and thread
Watercolor brush
Rubbing alcohol
 # 24 gauge white covered wire

 # 16 gauge wire for stems
Masking tape
Green floral tape

ADDITIONAL MATERIALS FOR LEAVES:

Chartreuse satin floral ribbon, 3" wide
Regular glue
 # 22 gauge green covered wire

Step-by-step for making daffodils:

Trace and transfer patterns to cardboard and cut out. Label patterns.

1. MAKE THE TRUMPET.

Cut center trumpet from taffeta.

With orange felt-tip marker, lightly touch the top rippled edge. With watercolor brush dipped in alcohol, touch the color, bleeding and softening it.

Glue the two ends of trumpet piece together forming a circle, then with needle and thread make a running stitch about ¼" from bottom. Draw thread up as tight as possible and tack. See illustration 1.

Invert the trumpet, then cut a desired length of #16 gauge stem wire. Make a small hook in one end. Place a drop of glue on the hook, then insert the wire into the center of the trumpet, catching the hook on the fabric inside. Allow to dry. See illustration 2.

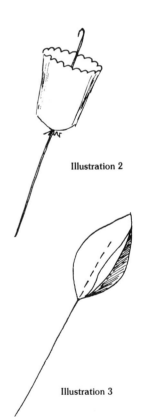

Illustration 2

Illustration 3

2. MAKE THE PETALS.

Cut 12 taffeta petals which will make six double petals.

Cut #24 gauge white covered wire into six 4" pieces.

Coat 1½" of wire with glue and sandwich, centered, between two petals, leaving uncoated end of wire extended at base for assembling. Allow to dry. See illustration 3.

With a very hot iron, touch each double petal with a quick, down-and-up motion. Test the technique on scraps first.

3. MAKE THE LEAVES.

Use the same leaf pattern and directions as shown for day lilies, again using chartreuse satin floral ribbon. Make two leaves for each flower. See instructions and Day Lily Illustrations 4 and 5, page 90.

4. ASSEMBLE THE DAFFODIL.

Place the six double petals around the base of the center trumpet already attached to the stem. Twist the extended petal wires around stem wire at base of the trumpet. Secure with masking tape. See illustration 4.

Wrap entire stem with floral tape, attaching leaves as you wrap. See illustration 5.

Illustration 4

Illustration 5

Johnny Jump-Ups

Color Plate 4

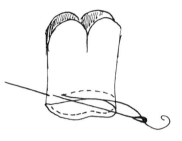

YOU WILL NEED:

Purple silk organza

Quick-sticking white glue

Needle and thread

 # 20 gauge wire for stem

Masking tape

Green floral tape

ADDITIONAL MATERIALS FOR LEAVES:

Sized medium green silklike fabric such as taffeta or sheath lining fabric

 # 26 gauge green covered wire

Regular glue

Illustration 1

Step-by-step for making johnny jump-ups:

🐝 Trace patterns, transfer to cardboard and cut out. Label each.

1. MAKE THE FLOWER PARTS.

🐝 Cut petals from purple silk organza.

🐝 Glue the two ends together to form a circle.

🐝 With a needle and thread, making a running stitch along base of petals about ¹/₈″ from bottom. Draw up tight and tack. See illustration 1.

🐝 Make a hook on one end of # 20 gauge wire cut to desired length. Cover the hook with floral tape, shaping into a tiny ball. See illustration 2.

🐝 Tear 2″ long pieces of masking tape into very narrow strips.

🐝 Insert stem into center of blossom, pulling wire down to position the covered hook in center of flower to serve as stamen. See illustration 3.

🐝 Secure the base of blossom to wire stem by wrapping with thin strips of masking tape. See illustration 4.

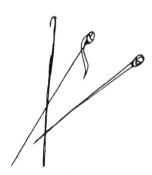

Illustration 2

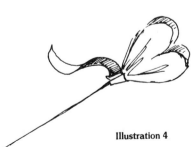

Illustration 4

Illustration 3

Patterns for Johnny Jump-up

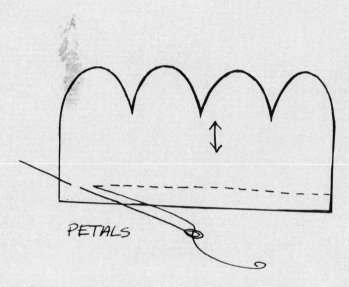

PETALS

LEAF

Arrow on pattern
indicates grain of fabric

2. MAKE THE LEAVES.

Cut two or three leaves for each flower from sized, medium green silklike fabric.

Stretch edges of leaves to shape.

Cut #26 gauge green covered wire into pieces about 2″ long.

Glue covered wire to center back of each leaf, leaving 1″ extended at base for attaching to stem. Allow to dry. See illustration 5.

Illustration 5

3. ASSEMBLE THE JOHNNY JUMP-UP.

Wrap entire stem with floral tape, attaching two or three leaves near top of stem as you wrap. See illustration 6.

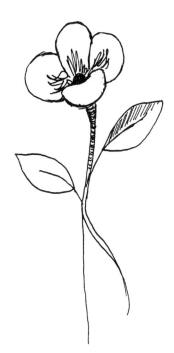

Illustration 6

Orange Silk Poppy

Color Plate 5

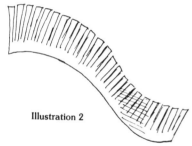

Illustration 1

Illustration 2

Illustration 3

YOU WILL NEED:

Sized orange semitransparent silklike fabric

Red felt-tip marker

Fine-line black felt-tip marker

Black felt for stamen

Bread dough (See recipe, page 31.)

A dab of green water-color, sap green if you buy it in the tube

Watercolor brush

Rubbing alcohol

Quick-sticking white glue

 # 16 gauge wire for stems

Masking tape

Green floral tape

ADDITIONAL MATERIALS FOR LEAVES AND FOR BUDS:

Sage green taffeta, sized (You really get a better look here if you dye the fabric — the alcohol applied later gives a more natural look.)

Yellow felt-tip marker

 # 22 gauge green covered wire

Cosmetic cotton balls

Step-by-step for making the poppy:

Trace and transfer patterns to cardboard and cut out. Label each.

1. MAKE THE STAMEN.

With dab of green watercolor, color bread dough a delicate sage green by working it into the dough.

Make a ball of dough the size of a large marble.

Put a hook on one end of # 16 gauge stem wire cut to desired length.

Apply glue to the hook, then insert into dough ball.

With a case knife or similar implement, make creases in the dough, radiating from center out to edges. See illustration 1. Allow to dry overnight.

When dry, use a fine-line felt-tip marker with permanent ink to color each crease in the dough black.

Cut a strip of black felt 1½″ by 8″ and fringe one edge within ³/₈″ of the other edge. See illustration 2.

Place glue on unfringed edge of strip and wind around wire at base of bread ball center. See illustration 3. Allow to dry.

2. MAKE THE PETALS.

🎨 Cut four small petals and five or six large petals for one flower.

🎨 Gently stretch the top edge of each petal.

🎨 With red felt-tip marker, color the very edges of petals, then with watercolor brush dipped in alcohol, bleed and blend the colors. See illustration 4.

🎨 With fingers, crease and pleat petals in ¹/₈″ pleats. See illustration 4.

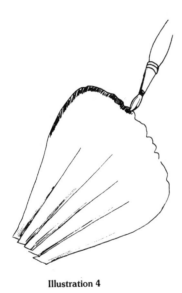

Illustration 4

3. MAKE THE LEAVES.

🎨 Make two or more leaves for each flower. From green taffeta cut two pieces for each leaf.

🎨 Cut #22 gauge green covered wire into 7″ lengths.

🎨 Coat about 5″ with glue. Sandwich wire between two leaf pieces leaving the uncoated 2″ extended for assembly. Let dry. See illustration 5.

🎨 With yellow marker, lightly draw veins on both sides of leaf.

🎨 With watercolor brush dipped in alcohol, touch the markings, bleeding and softening the color. Allow to dry.

Illustration 5

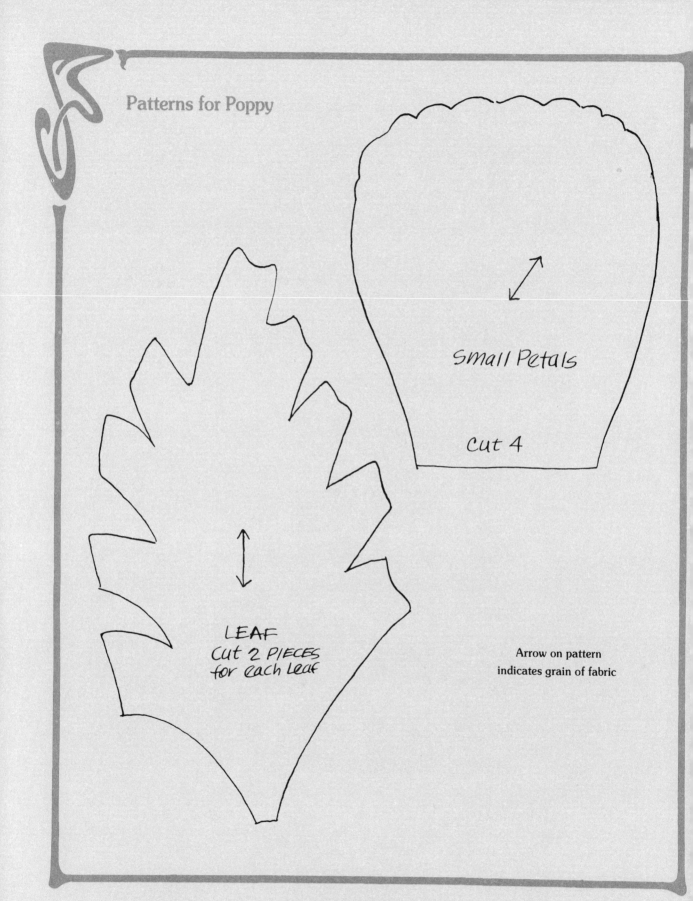

Patterns for Poppy

Small Petals

Cut 4

LEAF
Cut 2 PIECES
for each Leaf

Arrow on pattern
indicates grain of fabric

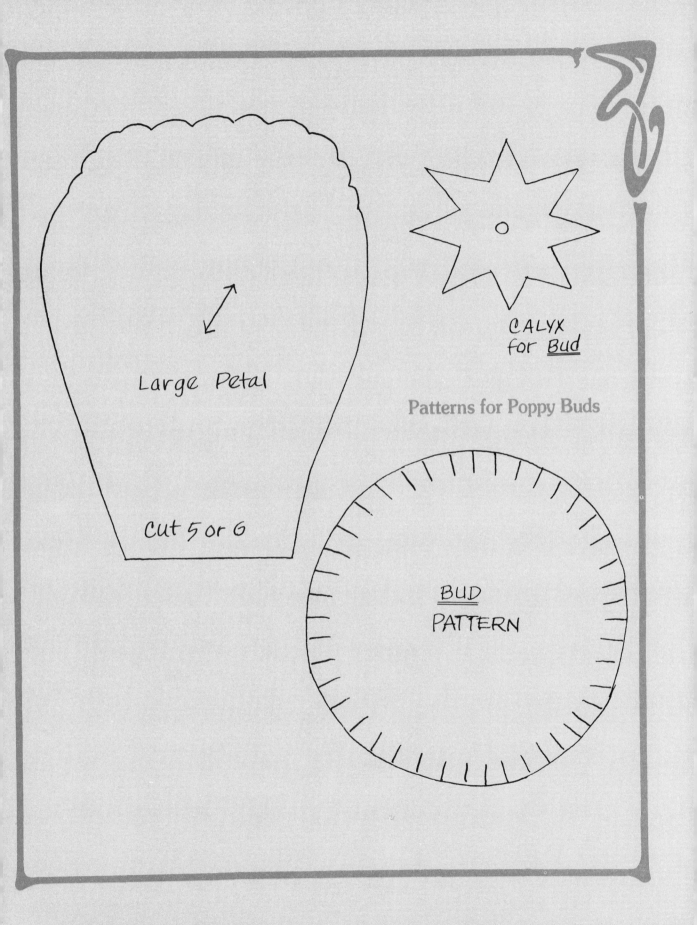

Large Petal

Cut 5 or 6

CALYX
for Bud

Patterns for Poppy Buds

BUD
PATTERN

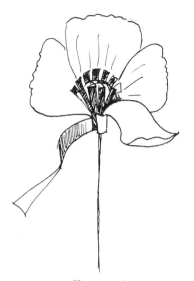

4. ASSEMBLE THE POPPY.

🎨 Tear off several narrow strips of masking tape 2″ or 3″ long.

🎨 Place four small petals equally spaced around the center stamens and tape into place with masking tape. See illustration 6.

🎨 Add five to six large petals, taping individually, if necessary, spacing evenly around center. Secure all petals firmly with masking tape.

🎨 Wrap entire stem with floral tape, attaching two small leaves and one or more large leaves to stem. See illustration 7.

Illustration 6

Illustration 7

5. MAKE BUDS FOR POPPY.

Cut bud pattern from orange silk. You may want to use two thicknesses if your fabric is very transparent.

Cut bud calyx from sized green leaf fabric.

Make a hook on one end of #16 gauge wire cut to desired length. Pull hook down through the cotton ball. Cover cotton ball with orange silk circle cut for bud, gather around base of cotton ball, and secure with a narrow strip of masking tape. See illustration 8.

Make a hole in the center of the calyx fabric. Place glue on inside of calyx. Insert stem of bud into center hole in calyx, bringing it up around base of bud, and then glue to bud. See illustration 9.

Wrap stem with floral tape, attaching a couple of small leaves. See illustration 9.

Illustration 8

Illustration 9

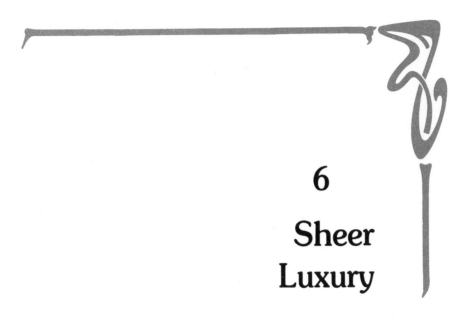

6

Sheer
Luxury

The rose and the lily . . . two flowers which add up to "sheer" (as in fabric) luxury. Searching for a term to describe the mood of these flowers, I came upon a new word. Well, it is not exactly new, but it is one seldom used in a conversation. The word is diaphanous. According to Webster, diaphanous is "characterized by fineness of texture . . . extreme delicacy of form." Another meaning of it is ethereal.

Diaphanous serves well to describe the rose and ethereal is an apt definition for the lily, but then I kept looking and found Webster defines luxury as "something adding to pleasure or comfort, something desirable, usually costly and unaffordable but not absolutely necessary."

Now, understand, I realize Mr. Webster's definitions were not directed personally at my chapter title and I'm not the least bit offended. But I think that possibly he did not understand flower fashioning. You see, the making of flowers, especially the diaphanous rose and the ethereal lily, only *appear* to be costly and beyond our reach. But, to take the first definition, by "being desirable and by adding pleasure and comfort," that is luxury, "Sheer Luxury." And is it not possible they could be necessary?

Of course, I am playing word games. Mr. Webster's point is well taken. But it does seem to me that sometimes there is a fine line between luxury, "not absolutely necessary," and luxury as it meets our psychological and emotional needs. Who can say we do not "need" a beautiful bouquet of

. . . the rose of Sharon, and the lily of the valley . . .

THE SONG OF SOLOMON

105

yellow roses or pink or white or red, which will neither fade nor wither before our mood does?

Roses have become the ultimate symbol of sentiment, the expression of love, often saying what words will not. They are universally accepted as the queen of beauty among flowers. They are usually so perfect as to be arrogant. Yet they offer themselves in almost feminine and masculine characteristics in order for us to use them in expressing ourselves. Combine dark red roses with eucalyptus or other heavy materials and they are becoming in the most masculine room. The pinks, yellows, and other pastels combined with a light, airy filler immediately suggest the feminine.

Having been born and reared "deep in the heart of" I would not be a true Texan if I didn't include in this book the Yellow Rose of. You can see it in Color Plate 6. There is a good chance you might not be sentimental about Texas—you had rather make your roses blush pink, blazing orange, or Valentine red and lace white. I can assure you they will be beautiful and far easier to make than you might expect. Dyeing your fabrics a variety of values, then lightly sizing them, makes this possible. These roses are a good example of the advantages of dyeing and sizing in flower fashioning.

At the other end of flower making techniques is the silk lily, uncolored, unsized. It is shown in Color Plate 7. This flower offers an unlimited challenge of your artistic hand.

I have such a love affair with flowers that I have found each time I have started to tell how to make a certain one I was tempted to say it was my "favorite." There was always, however, a certain reservation. Now is the time!

While the lily is not necessarily my favorite fresh flower, it has to be the most exciting to make. You may have noticed I have included in this book those made from silk organza designed in an Oriental line arrangement, some tiny ones made from satin as in the bridal bouquet, some from taffeta included with the spring bulb flowers, and some made of brown paper sacks in the chapter **Unlikely Etceteras.** I just couldn't resist including one last one made of white dotted swiss shown in the bridal picture.

Lilies are a personality flower, adding something special to many arrangements with their distinctive shape and markings. They are unquestionably one of the easiest of all to make—six petals, six stamens. But the wide variety of personality makes it possible to fashion them out of practically anything you have on hand. They especially lend themselves well to hand painting.

The exotic white and green silk lilies in Color Plate 7 use a technique not suggested elsewhere in this book. The edges of the petals are rolled. It is a

106

simple, easy technique. It offers a soft, natural, yet fragile, appearance. There is, however, one aspect of it you should know and remember. It does not work well using a fabric with high nylon or polyester content. These synthetics seem to make the fabric very stubborn and resistant to rolling. It can be done, but it is too tedious to be satisfying. Therefore, be sure you have purchased a silk organza which is only rayon and silk. Cotton organdy also works well, as does chiffon which is lightly sized.

The fun of this flower is in the decoration. Choose your color. Dye white organza if necessary. Then, after it is assembled, be the artist with a watercolor brush and with little dabs of dye water. Give it whatever personality you like: soft pink with dark maroon and red speckles, or perhaps make it a real tiger lily, soft burnt orange with black and brown spots.

JAN WALKER

Organdy Rose

Color Plate 6

A memo to Flower Fashioners. Instructions for sizing fabrics, page 28. Directions for covering wire, page 31. Bread dough recipe, page 31.

YOU WILL NEED:

Organdy dyed several shades of yellow, sized (Reserve enough organdy unsized in darker shades for buds and centers.)

Medium green cotton for calyx, sized

#16 gauge stem wire

Quick-sticking white glue

Masking tape

Green floral tape

ADDITIONAL MATERIALS FOR LEAVES:

#22 gauge wire

Green satin floral ribbon, 2¼" wide

Regular glue

Green felt-tip marker

Step-by-step for making rose:

Trace patterns, transfer to cardboard and cut out. Label each.

1. MAKE THE FLOWER PARTS.

To make centers and bud, bend a small hook at one end of #16 gauge wire cut to desired length for stem.

For each bud and center, cut a strip of unsized fabric 4½" by 8". Lightly fold in half lengthwise but do not crease. See illustration 1.

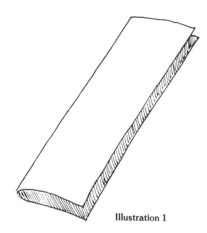

Illustration 1

Hold end of folded strip between the thumb and index finger of your left hand; with your right hand, roll strip loosely around thumb and finger to form roll. See illustration 2.

Insert the stem wire through the center of roll and pull the hook down to catch on the fabric inside the roll. Pinch the bottom of the roll together and attach to stem wire with masking tape. See illustration 3.

Cut seven to nine petals out of sized organdy for each rose. I usually cut about four from the same color I am using for the bud, then about five out of a shade very *slightly* lighter.

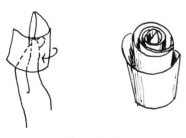

Illustration 2

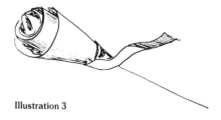

Illustration 3

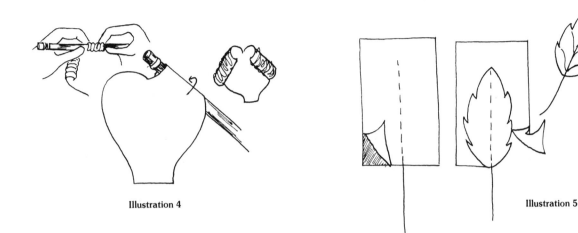

Illustration 4   Illustration 5

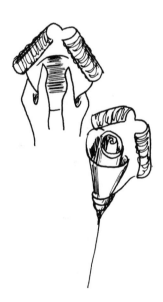

Illustration 6

❀ With a pencil, roll the upper curved edge of each petal to the indentation. While still on the pencil, push the ends of the rolled edges in toward each other to "crimp" the fabric. Remove pencil and set petals aside. See illustration 4.

2. MAKE THE LEAVES.

❀ Make three small leaves and one or two large leaves for each rose.

❀ For small leaves, cut #22 gauge wire into 5″ lengths and cut two pieces of green floral ribbon 3½″ long.

❀ For large leaves, cut #22 gauge wire into 6″ lengths and cut two pieces of green floral ribbon 4½″ long.

❀ Coat wrong side of one ribbon with glue. Sandwich the two ribbons, wrong sides together, with a wire between, leaving 2″ extended at base. Dry, then center pattern on ribbon and cut out. See illustration 5.

❀ With green felt-tip marker lightly stroke veins onto leaf.

3. ASSEMBLE THE ROSE.

❀ Gently cup the middle of one petal with your thumbs, the rolled edge facing *inward*. Pinch and pleat the petal base and glue it to the base of the center roll (bud) on the stem wire. See illustration 6.

❀ Add two or three more petals in this way.

109

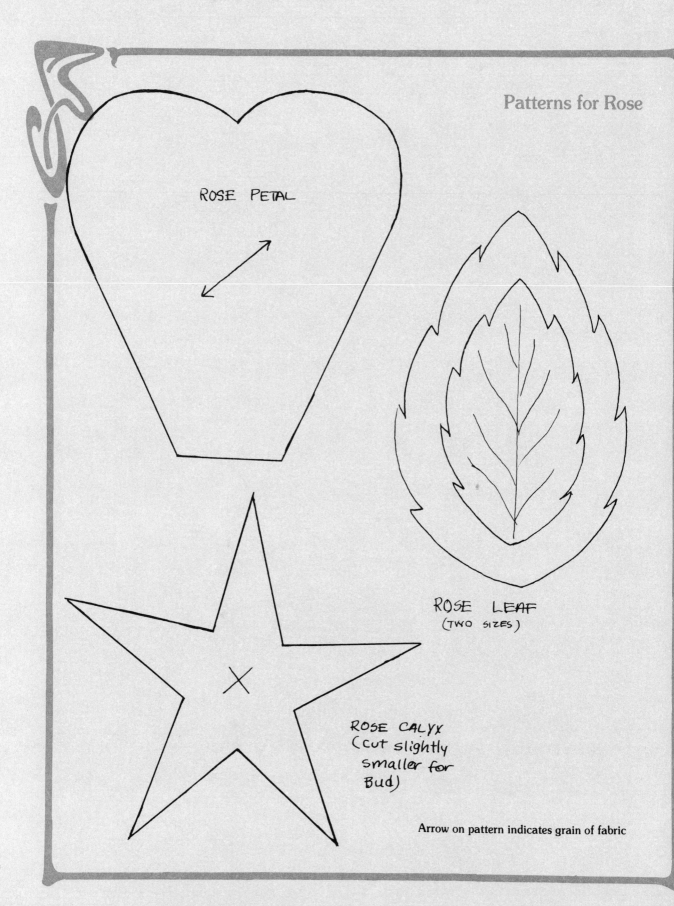

Patterns for Rose

ROSE PETAL

ROSE LEAF
(TWO SIZES)

ROSE CALYX
(cut slightly
smaller for
Bud)

Arrow on pattern indicates grain of fabric

Then glue on an outer layer of petals (slightly lighter in color), cupping the petals *outward* with your thumbs and gluing them with the rolled edges facing *outward*. See illustration 7.

Use a total of about nine petals for a full-blown rose and six for a smaller, partially open, rose.

Cut calyx from green cotton. Cut a cross in the center.

Insert stem of rose into cross of calyx. Place glue on inside of calyx, pull up on stem and position around the base of rose.

Wrap entire stem with green floral tape, attaching three small leaves near top, one or more large leaves lower on stem. See illustration 8.

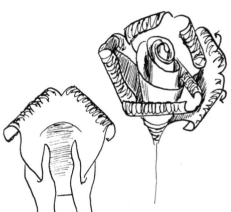

Illustration 7

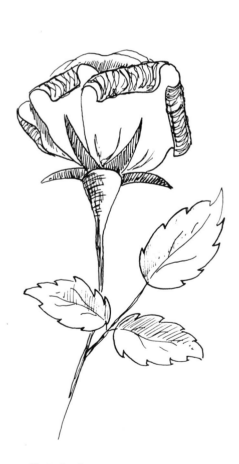

Illustration 8

White Silk Lily

Color Plate 7

YOU WILL NEED:

White rayon and silk organza (Be sure it does not contain nylon or polyester.)

Bread dough for stamen (See recipe, page 31.)

 # 24 gauge white covered wire for petals

 # 26 gauge green covered wire for stamens

 # 16 gauge wire for stems

Quick-sticking white glue

Small watercolor brush

Olive green fabric dye for decorating

Masking tape

Green floral tape

ADDITIONAL MATERIALS FOR LEAVES:

Avocado green satin floral ribbon

 # 22 gauge wire

Regular glue

Step-by-step for making a lily:

Trace patterns, transfer to cardboard and cut out. Label each.

1. MAKE THE PETALS.

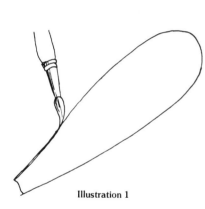

Illustration 1

Cut six petals for each flower from white silk organza. (Silk organza is a "crawly" fabric, and I have found it convenient to thumb-tack the material to my sizing board or bread board, then mark around pattern and cut out while tacked to the board.)

To roll petal edges, mix a small amount of glue and water to a thin consistency. With watercolor brush, brush glue on the very edge of petals. See illustration 1. While still "tacky," roll the edges toward you between thumb and forefinger of both hands, stretching as you roll. (I find I often instinctively dampen my thumb with my tongue as I do this. This principle is the same as the old hand-rolled hems you used to see on handkerchiefs.) See illustration 2.

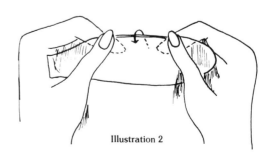

Illustration 2

112

Pattern for Petal/Lily

● For leaf pattern, use iris leaf pattern on page 77.

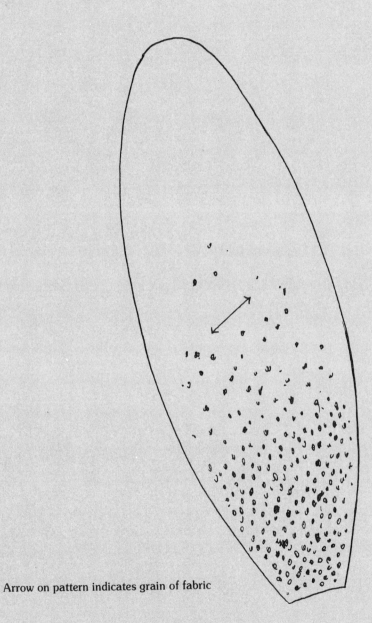

Arrow on pattern indicates grain of fabric

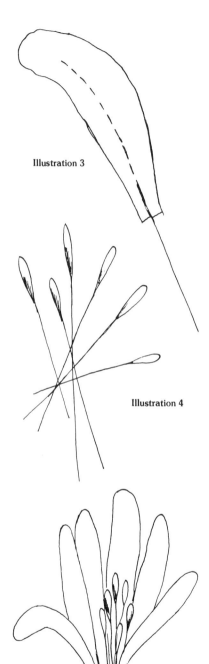

Illustration 3

Illustration 4

Illustration 5

To attach support wires, cut #24 gauge white covered wire into 8" lengths.

Run your thumb and forefinger down length of wire to slightly curve it. Coat about 5½" with glue and very carefully attach to back of petal (rolled edges face to the top), leaving the balance of wire extended at base of petal. Avoid getting excess glue on the silk. Lay aside to dry. See illustration 3.

2. MAKE THE STAMENS.

Cut six pieces of #26 gauge green covered wire 5" long.

Glue to one end of each wire a piece of bread dough the size of a pea. Roll between fingers, then flatten slightly. Allow to harden. See illustration 4.

3. MAKE THE LEAVES.

For each leaf, cut two pieces of avocado green floral ribbon and one 12" length of #22 gauge green covered wire.

Coat wrong side of one ribbon with regular glue.

Center the wire on the glue and sandwich the two ribbons, wrong sides together, with wire between, leaving 2" extended at one end for attaching to stem. Allow to dry. See instructions, and Tulip Illustration 4, page 74.

Center leaf pattern on wired ribbon and cut out shape.

4. ASSEMBLE AND DECORATE THE LILY.

Place six stamens in the center of six petals and twist all the extended base wires together. See illustration 5.

Cut #16 gauge stem wire into desired lengths. Lay alongside the twisted petal wires and secure with masking tape.

To decorate, shape petals into lily form, then mix a small amount of olive green dye, a somewhat weak diluted solution, then another small amount of a stronger, deeper color, almost black looking.

With watercolor brush dipped in weaker solution, speckle and freckle the lily with a heavier concentration of speckles near the center, decreasing to just a few spots near the tips of petals. Let dry completely. See illustration 6.

To emphasize coloring, after first speckle job is dry, with the brush

dipped in deeper colored dye, go over same area, using half as many speckles. Dry.

 Wrap stem with green floral tape, attaching leaves near bottom of stem as you wrap. See illustration 6.

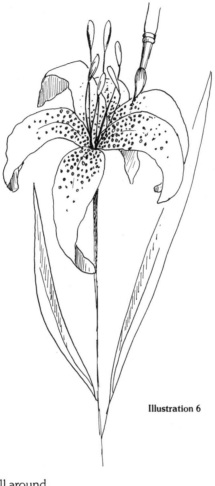

Illustration 6

Illustration 7

5. MAKE THE BUDS.

 Reduce petal pattern by ¼" all around.

Cut four petals for each bud.

Twist the stem of four petals together, facing inward, and secure with masking tape.

Shape petals by cupping them inward.

Wrap stem with floral tape, attaching a couple of leaves as you wrap. See illustration 7.

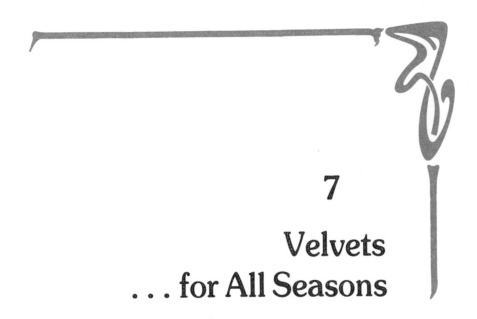

7

Velvets
... for All Seasons

Velvet is a storybook fabric. It is what you "dress up in" when you go do something glamorous and romantic. Remember when you were a child? There was the Fairy Princess, dancing on tiny velvet shoes, adorned in her robe of brilliant velvet. There was her Prince Charming, resplendent in his velvet doublet and knee breeches. He may have been shod in velvet, too. Certainly you recall Scarlett O'Hara. Before the War between the States, Scarlett — unless it was a hot summer's evening — was gowned in antebellum velvet when she came whirling down the stairway at Tara to join the dancing. You knew she would be, even if you only saw *Gone With the Wind* eight times. Velvet was Napoleon Bonaparte before Elba and it was all the kings and queens and dukes. Velvet was and is the cloth of papal splendor, the fabric of the hierarchy. It symbolizes ritual and feudal splendor. It is royal and regal. You may or may not be a romanticist, but when I take scissors to a piece of velvet or velveteen I am overwhelmed, exhilarated by the very feel of the fabric. It has what some describe as "hand," an exquisite nap, a supple, downy, fibrous surface which is awesome.

Velvet and velveteen are highly versatile fabrics for flower fashioning. They are an ideal material for leaves as well as petals. Many live leaves look as if they are fashioned of velvet. Recently the possibility of sizing velvet and velveteen challenged me to experiment a bit. It worked! A whole new world of flower making opened up! Size the fabric, brushing glue on the back, dry

If eyes were made for seeing,
Then beauty is its own excuse for being.
EMERSON

117

it, cut out whatever shape you wish. It will hold the design you decree. It will not ravel. The sizing permits you to pull and stretch the edges, giving petals and leaves realistic dimensions. Its versatility extends to flowers of almost any type. White velvet suggests the appearance of translucence well enough to be a lily, or pink velvet a part of a sweet pea. The "hand" or soft nap of the fabric is especially receptive to subtle colorations supplied with felt-tip markers and acrylic and oil paints. Or, left alone, as in a creamy white gardenia, the natural lights and darks of the nap may need no further help from you to make it appear lifelike. Velvet bespeaks regency.

You will find here patterns for four velvet flowers. Each of the four has a distinct shape, each its own characteristics. And the four depict seasons of the year. First is the stately tulip, a lofty flower, one which is among the first to greet us in the spring. Then there is the pansy, a dainty flower which might be called cute. Pansies bloom early and they bloom and bloom right through the summer. Also pictured is an off-white gardenia, just right for you to wear to the first dance of autumn. Finally, velvet as a holiday blossom, a poinsettia to brighten your home during the Yuletide. All these flowers are pictured in color Plates 8, 9, 10, and 11.

The tulips, with all their imposing dignity, were made before I discovered sizing, but the technique used in them has other advantages. Both

front and back of each petal are of velvet. The two pieces are glued together, a wire between them, making it possible to decorate the inside and the outside of the petal. This decoration makes them attractive shown full-blown. Or, if you wish, you can bend three of the petals downward and three upward, giving the shape of an iris.

The pansy is summer's tiny flower. It is synonymous with children. An avid gardener I know has her pansy bed out front, an invitation to the children to stop and gather some for their mothers. Once she overheard some of them shouting in delight, "Come on! Here's where we can pick the chim-pansies!' " Not a bad description. Have you ever looked a pansy square in the face? Notice how it looks like a person — or a chimpanzee? Examine one. Can you see the eyes, the nose? Children delight in looking for the face.

Summer's almost gone. Fall is drawing nigh. So make the creamy white velveteen gardenia, totally as romantic, if not as fragrant, as the real thing. (You could plan on always wearing a popular gardenia scented perfume when wearing your hand-fashioned blooms!) Make them to pin at the throat of your new fall chiffon gown, on the shoulder of a velvet evening cloak, on

the belt of a street-length cocktail dress. Or, if you prefer not to wear them, pin one to an evening bag. Perhaps you will take those precious scraps of fake suede from the shirtwaist you've just sewn and fashion them into a matching blossom for your dress. Give it the chic of the designer models, a touch of class.

Finally we come to the velvet poinsettia, a blossom for the holidays. This flower is an import, brought to us from neighbors in Mexico and South America. It has come to be a part of our lives, just as the other Latin influences which enrich our architecture, language, diet, and decorating.

The potted poinsettia is a tradition when many households are dressed for holiday visitors. Keep the live ones, certainly. But consider adapting the blossom itself, making it in various sizes for use about the house. But please, no plastics! Plastic poinsettias scream "commercial" and more commercial greetings we do not need. The pink, dark red, red-orange and almost green white of the plants are too lovely to try to imitate with plastic reproductions. Poinsettias call for velvet, rich, warm, beautiful velvet.

This year try something different. Use velvet blossoms along with banks of potted live poinsettias at your doorway or at the foot of a staircase. Make poinsettias of various sizes and weave them into a centerpiece for a table. Add them to the wreath above your fireplace. Use them individually as decorations for the tree or as package ornaments. Attach them to rich greenery swags for the mantle or the banister. Pile a few in a nice wicker basket and combine with pine boughs and a big red bow for the hearth of a favorite friend. Do start early because you will want to make more and more of them to give away. Rarely is anything more appreciated than a well-done, fashionable gift made with the love of your own hands and with your precious time. It is a truly lovely way to say, "Happy holidays!"

Look carefully at a live poinsettia and you will discover they have various numbers and sizes of petals. The "petals" are in fact "bracts." The *blossom* is actually the little greenish yellow buds in the center. But here we will do a bit of cheating. So as not to confuse you by changing terminology, let us stick to "petals" for the blossom or bracts. And we'll treat those small yellow buds as the stamens. A specific number of petals is given for each velvet poinsettia, but do not feel confined. If you want to add another small or large petal, for heaven's sake, do not be timid. Add or subtract what is required to make the blossom acceptable to you. If you lack confidence, examine a live one. If no fresh poinsettia is available, look at some old Christmas cards for pictures to copy. You say you don't have last year's Christmas cards! I can't imagine! Okay, then. You will have to take my word.

These are the flowers for the seasons—tulips, pansies, gardenias, poinsettias. Some day soon I hope to add another one. It will be for a fifth season—oil painting on velvet. Velvet takes well to oils. Some of you may have already tried this technique. You know the oil-on-velvet paintings you see peddlers hawking in border towns from California to Texas? Some of them may be good but most are pretty dreadful. The technique has some merit though, and some day soon I am going to tackle velvet flowers with paints and see how I come out. There would be a flower, indeed. Olé! Olé!

The Velvet Tulip

Color Plate 3 (As seen in Family Circle Magazine)

YOU WILL NEED:

Velveteen in "strong" yellow, deep pink, lavender, and orange, unsized

Felt-tip markers in green, yellow, orange, purple, and red

Rubbing alcohol and cotton pad

Regular white glue (Slomon's Sobo fabric glue works well here.)

Bread dough (See recipe, page 31.)

 # 22 gauge green covered wire

 # 16 gauge wire for stems

Masking tape

Floral tape

ADDITIONAL MATERIAL FOR LEAVES.

Bright moss green velveteen

A memo to Flower Fashioners. Instructions for sizing fabrics, page 28. Directions for covering wire, page 31. Bread dough recipe, page 31.

Illustration 1

Step-by-step for making tulip:

Trace and transfer patterns to cardboard and cut out. Label each.

1. MAKE THE FLOWER PARTS.

Make three stamens for each tulip. Cut # 22 gauge green covered wire into 5″ lengths. To one end of each wire glue a ball of bread dough the size of a large pea, flattened out to elongate. Allow to harden, then paint yellow with a felt-tip marker. See illustration 1.

Each tulip has four large and two small petals. For each petal, cut two pieces of velveteen 3½″ by 5″ and one piece of # 22 gauge green covered wire 5″ long.

Coat wrong side of one square of velveteen with glue. Center wire on velveteen leaving 1½″ extended at bottom. Lay the other piece of velveteen, wrong side down, on top of glue-covered piece, thus bonding the two pieces together with the wire sandwiched in between. See illustration 2. Allow to dry.

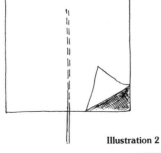

Illustration 2

123

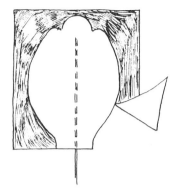

Illustration 3

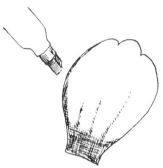

Illustration 4

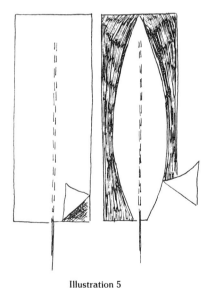

Illustration 5

🎨 Center pattern on top of square and cut out. See illustration 3.

🎨 With felt-tip markers, shade petals by stroking lightly from the base of petal outward toward tip, making heavier markings at base. See illustration 4. On the yellow tulip, use yellow and green markers. On the pink, use orange. On the lavender, use purple. On the orange, use yellow and red or orange.

🎨 Blend and soften the markings with a little alcohol on a cotton pad.

2. MAKE THE LEAVES.

🎨 For large leaf, cut two pieces of fabric 9″ by 2½″ and for small leaf cut two pieces 7″ by 2″.

🎨 Cut #22 gauge green covered wire into 9″ lengths for large leaf, 7″ for small leaf.

🎨 Coat wrong side of one fabric piece with glue. Center a piece of wire on glue leaving 1½″ extended at base to attach to stem. Top with other fabric piece, wrong side down, bonding the wire between the fabric pieces. Allow to dry. See illustration 5.

🎨 Center pattern on the wired fabric and cut out. See illustration 5.

🎨 Decorate leaves in same manner you did flower petals. With green marker, stroke markings on the leaf, heavier at base, lighter toward the tip. See illustration 6.

3. ASSEMBLE THE TULIP.

🎨 Position two small petals around three stamens and four large petals around these.

🎨 Twist all stem wires together and secure with masking tape. See illustration 7.

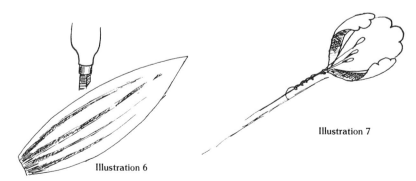

Illustration 6

Illustration 7

Patterns for Tulip

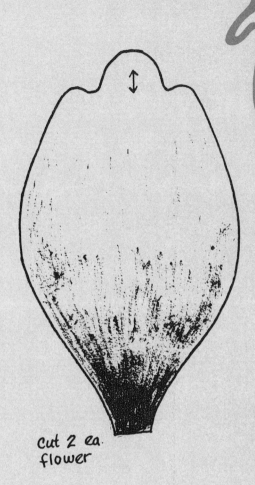

cut 2 ea.
flower

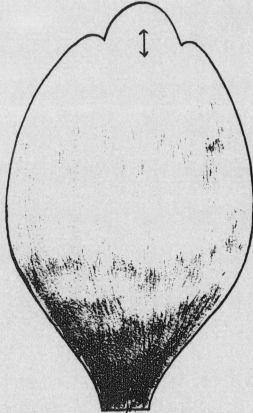

cut 4 for each flower

Arrow on pattern indicates grain of fabric

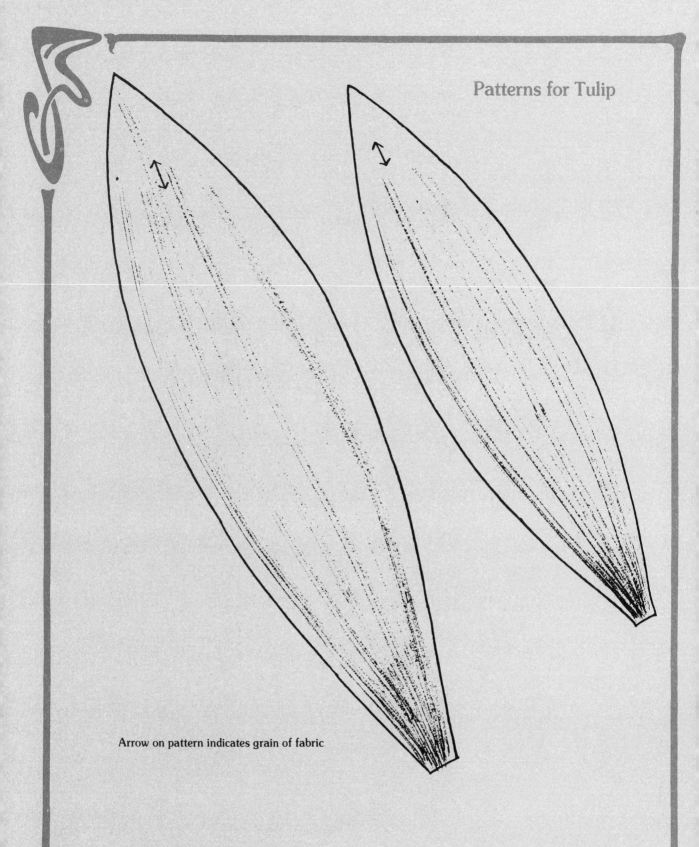

Patterns for Tulip

Arrow on pattern indicates grain of fabric

Cut #16 gauge stem wire into desired lengths. Lay alongside twisted petal stems and fasten with masking tape.

Wrap entire stem with floral tape, attaching one small and one large leaf low on the stem. See illustration 8.

Shape into tulip by cupping and bending two smaller center petals toward each other around stamens, then cupping the four larger petals around it likewise. See illustration 8. An iris shape can also be achieved by cupping the two center petals toward each other, bending the back petal up and the three remaining petals curved downward.

To effect a closed bud-type flower, assemble together four small petals cupping them inward. See illustration 9.

After tulip is finished and shaped, color the base of the petals on the inside of the flower near the stamens a deeper shade with a felt-tip marker.

Illustration 9

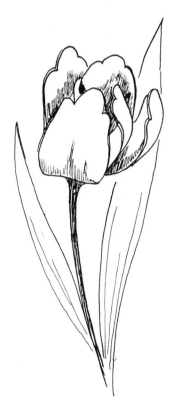

Illustration 8

127

Velvet Pansies

Color Plate 9

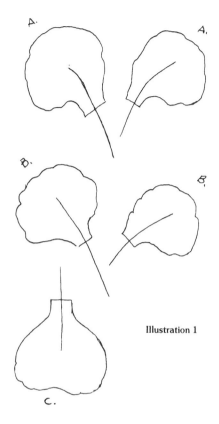

Illustration 1

YOU WILL NEED:

Dark red, purple, and yellow velvet, sized
Black and purple felt-tip markers
Tube of cadmium yellow acrylic paint
Bread dough (See recipe, page 31.)
Quick-sticking white glue
 # 24 gauge green covered wire

 # 16 gauge wire for stems
Masking tape
Green floral tape

ADDITIONAL MATERIAL FOR LEAVES:

Medium green velvet, sized

Step-by-step for making pansy:

Trace and transfer patterns to cardboard and cut out. Label each. Note the pattern instructions for reversing pattern in cutting some petals. There are five petals for each flower. See illustration 1.

1. MAKE THE FLOWER PARTS.

Cut #24 gauge green covered wire into pieces about 2" longer than each petal.

Coat about 1½" of each wire with glue. Attach to center back of each petal, allowing balance of wire to extend at base for assembly. Allow to dry. See illustration 2.

To make stamens, glue a ball of bread dough about the size of a small pea to a 3½" piece of #24 gauge green covered wire. Allow to harden. Then paint with yellow paint. See illustration 3.

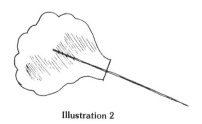

Illustration 2

Illustration 3

Velvet Pansies

Instructions for the pansy, page 128.

COLOR PLATE 10

Velvet Gardenias

Instructions for the gardenia, page 139.

ARRANGED BY DUSTY McGUIRE

Velvet Poinsettias

Instructions for poinsettia, page 142.

COLOR PLATE 12

Tooling Foil Poppies

Instructions for poppy, page 161.

AS SEEN IN **FAMILY CIRCLE**

COLOR PLATE 13

Kitchen Bouquet

Instructions for aluminum foil rose, page 150
tiger lily, page 154; aster, page 156;
white bean flower, page 160.

COLOR PLATE 14

Veneer Zinnias

Instructions for zinnia, page 164.

AS SEEN IN **FAMILY CIRCLE**

COLOR PLATE 15

Bridal Keepsakes

*Instructions for floribunda roses,
page 172 and 175; organdy roses,
page 175; chiffon rosebud,
page 176; satin lily, page 178.*

ARRANGED BY MARGIE BAST

(overleaf)
COLOR PLATE 16

Permanent Pot Plants

*Instructions for geranium,
page 185; hydrangea,
page 189; violet, page
192; begonia, page 195.*

A.

Cut 1, Reverse and
Cut another

B.

Cut 1, Reverse
and cut another

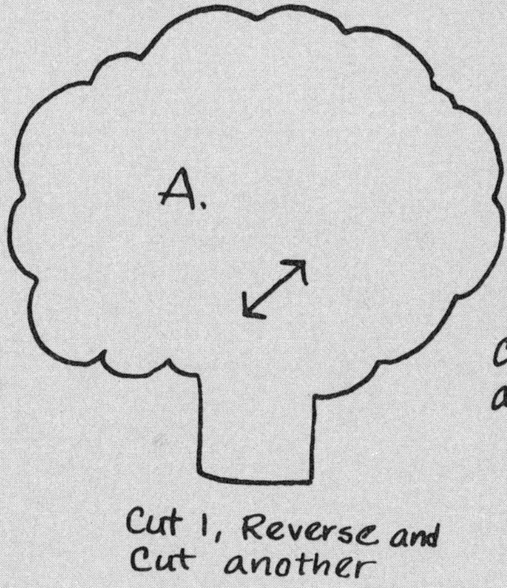

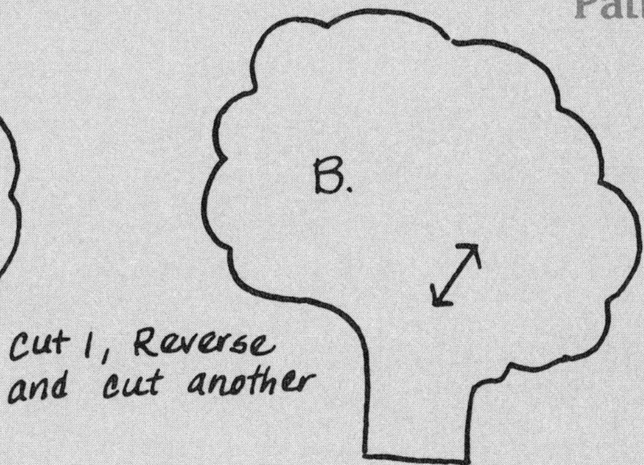

Arrow on pattern
indicates grain of fabric

C.

Cut 1

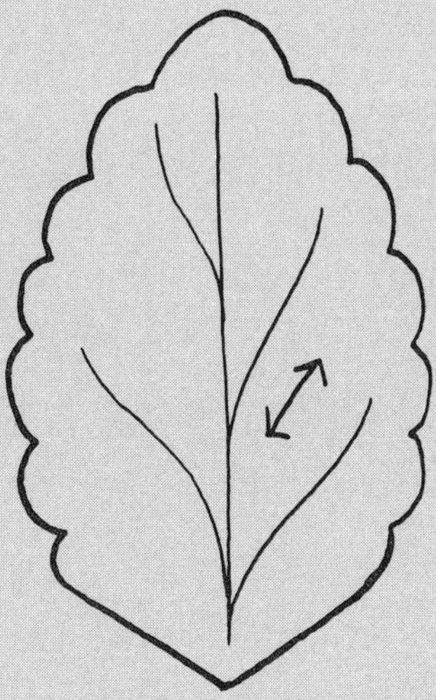

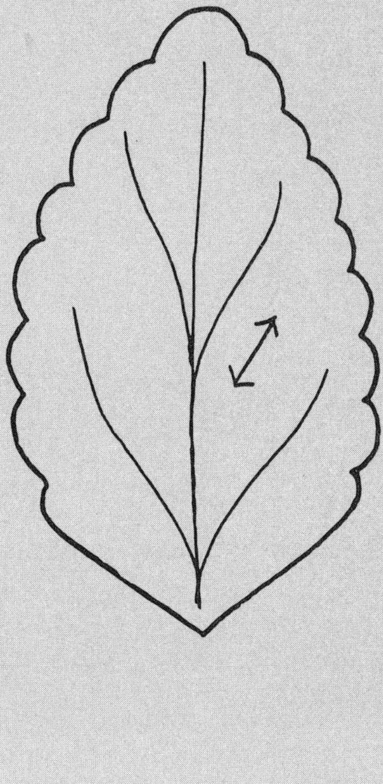

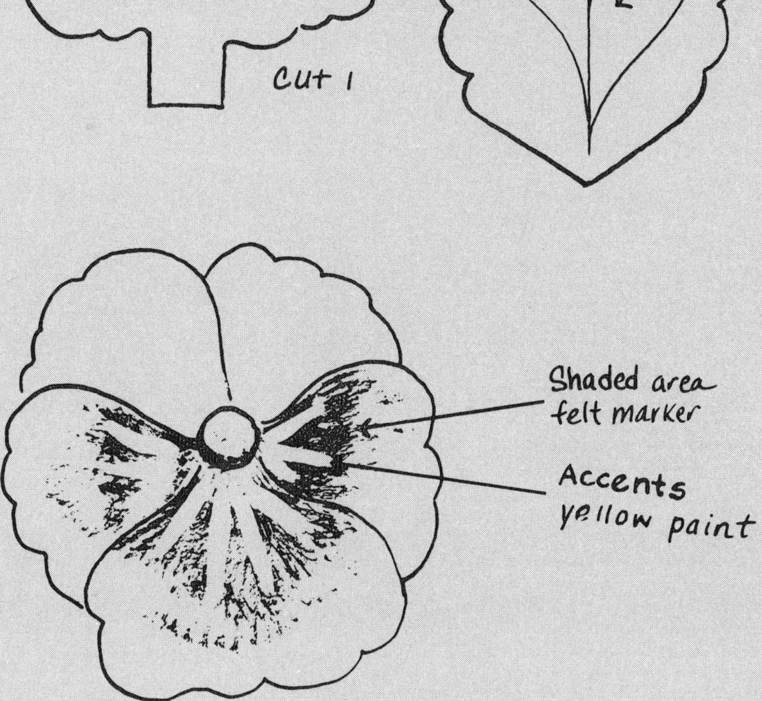

Shaded area
felt marker

Accents
yellow paint

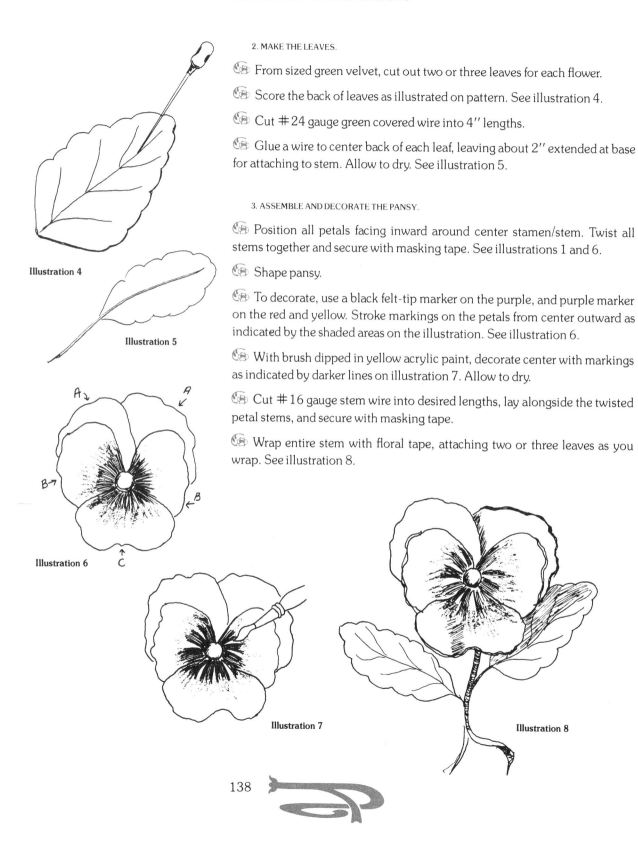

2. MAKE THE LEAVES.

🎨 From sized green velvet, cut out two or three leaves for each flower.

🎨 Score the back of leaves as illustrated on pattern. See illustration 4.

🎨 Cut #24 gauge green covered wire into 4″ lengths.

🎨 Glue a wire to center back of each leaf, leaving about 2″ extended at base for attaching to stem. Allow to dry. See illustration 5.

3. ASSEMBLE AND DECORATE THE PANSY.

🎨 Position all petals facing inward around center stamen/stem. Twist all stems together and secure with masking tape. See illustrations 1 and 6.

🎨 Shape pansy.

🎨 To decorate, use a black felt-tip marker on the purple, and purple marker on the red and yellow. Stroke markings on the petals from center outward as indicated by the shaded areas on the illustration. See illustration 6.

🎨 With brush dipped in yellow acrylic paint, decorate center with markings as indicated by darker lines on illustration 7. Allow to dry.

🎨 Cut #16 gauge stem wire into desired lengths, lay alongside the twisted petal stems, and secure with masking tape.

🎨 Wrap entire stem with floral tape, attaching two or three leaves as you wrap. See illustration 8.

Illustration 4

Illustration 5

Illustration 6

Illustration 7

Illustration 8

138

Gardenias

Color Plate 10

YOU WILL NEED:

Off-white velveteen, sized

Quick-sticking white glue

 # 24 gauge white covered wire

 # 16 gauge stem wire

Masking tape

Green floral tape

ADDITIONAL MATERIALS FOR LEAVES:

Bright green velvet, sized

 # 24 gauge green covered wire

Step-by-step for making gardenia:

Trace patterns, transfer to cardboard and cut out. Label each.

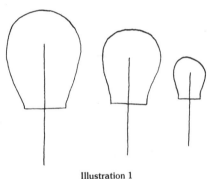

Illustration 1

1. MAKE THE PETALS.

For each large blossom, cut six large petals, six medium and six small petals. For small blossom, cut six medium and six small petals. Pull and stretch the sides of petals.

Cut # 24 gauge white covered wire into lengths 3½″ long.

Glue a wire to center back of each petal, gluing the end just slightly past the center of petal. See illustration 1. Allow the balance of wire to extend at base for assembling. Allow to dry.

2. MAKE THE LEAVES.

For one large and one small blossom, cut about four large leaves and three small leaves.

Score the back of leaves as indicated on pattern. Pull and stretch sides to improve shape. See illustration 2.

Cut # 24 gauge green covered wire into 7″ pieces.

Glue wire piece to center back of each leaf, leaving balance of wire extended at base, for attaching to flower stem. See illustration 3.

Illustration 2

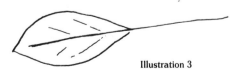

Illustration 3

139

3. ASSEMBLE THE GARDENIA.

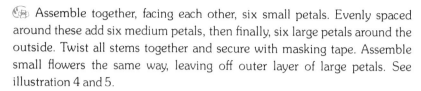

🎨 Assemble together, facing each other, six small petals. Evenly spaced around these add six medium petals, then finally, six large petals around the outside. Twist all stems together and secure with masking tape. Assemble small flowers the same way, leaving off outer layer of large petals. See illustration 4 and 5.

🎨 Cut a piece of 16″ gauge wire about 6″ long. Lay alongside twisted stem wires and secure with masking tape.

🎨 Wrap twisted stems of smaller blossom with floral tape.

🎨 Wrap stem of larger flower with floral tape, attaching just below blossom two large leaves and one small leaf, cutting the stems as necessary to have them extend beyond the blossom.

🎨 Continue wrapping stem with floral tape, then attach the small blossom about half way down on the stem. Again, add two or three leaves. See illustration 6.

🎨 Bend and curve balance of stem wire.

Illustration 4

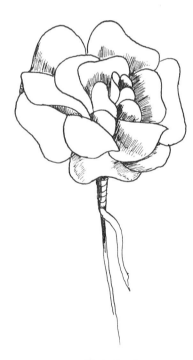

Illustration 5

Illustration 6

Patterns for Gardenia

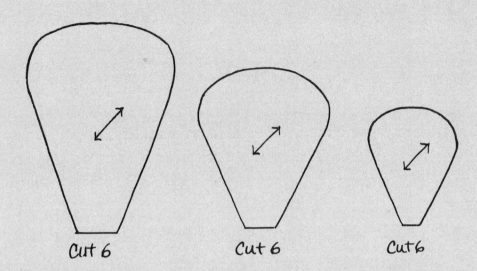

Cut 6   Cut 6   Cut 6

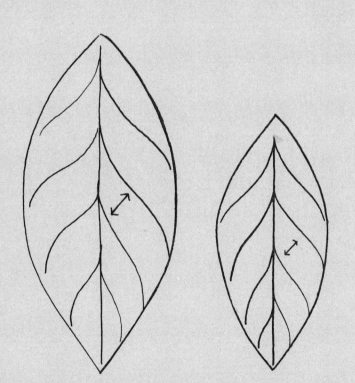

Arrow on pattern
indicates grain of fabric

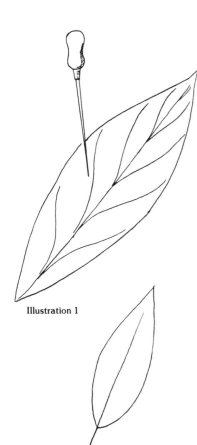

Illustration 1

Illustration 2

Poinsettia

Color Plate 11

YOU WILL NEED:

Bright red velvet, sized (Or, use pink or green-white.) Either rayon or nylon velvet is acceptable, but make it velvet rather than velveteen.

Green pipe cleaners (Not chenille stems, which are too big in diameter, but actual pipe cleaners. Dip them in dye if you cannot find the right color.)

Small pea-sized gold beads (I buy strings of Christmas beads and unstring them. If you prefer your poinsettias to look less
ornamental and more realistic, attach pea-sized balls of bread dough on the ends of stems and decorate them with a yellow felt-tip marker.)

Quick-sticking white glue

 # 22 gauge red covered wire

 # 16 gauge stem wire

Masking tape

Green floral tape

Step-by-step for making a poinsetta:

Trace and transfer patterns to cardboard and cut out. Label each.

1. MAKE THE FLOWER PARTS.

Cut three sizes of petals for each poinsettia, about six small, four medium and six large petals. With ice pick, score veins on the reverse side of petals as indicated on the pattern. See illustration 1. This will leave a nice suggestion of veins in the velvet on the top side.

Cut # 22 gauge red covered wire into pieces 2″ longer than the petals.

With quick-sticking glue, attach a wire to the back of each petal, leaving about 2″ extended at base for assembly. Allow to dry. See illustration 2.

To make stamens, prepare six stamen pieces for each flower. Cut green pipe cleaners into pieces 2½″ long. Glue a gold Christmas bead to the end of each piece of pipe cleaner. Allow to dry. See illustration 3.

2. ASSEMBLE THE POINSETTIA.

Tear off two or three pieces of masking tape about 2″ long and then tear them lengthwise into strips about ¼″ wide. You need tiny, narrow strips of tape.

Twist bases of the six stamens together for the center.

Illustration 3

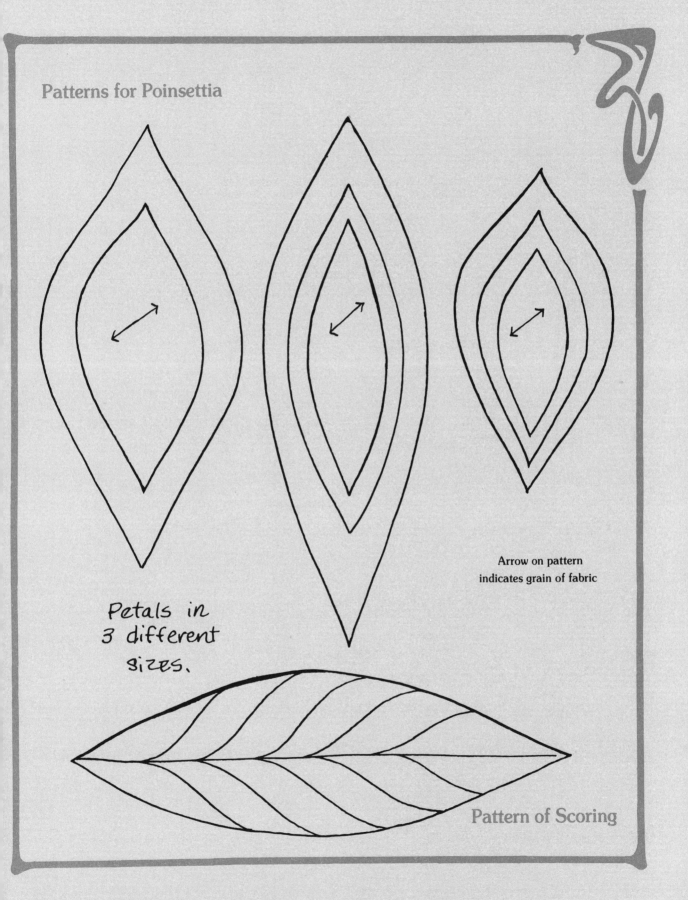

Patterns for Poinsettia

Arrow on pattern
indicates grain of fabric

Petals in
3 different
sizes.

Pattern of Scoring

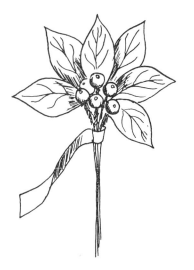

Illustration 4

🌀 Space the six small petals evenly around the center stamen. Secure the wires of the petals to the center with masking tape. See illustration 4.

🌀 In the same manner, evenly space six or seven larger petals around the center and secure with tape.

🌀 With masking tape, add four or five medium-sized petals, filling in any gaps. See illustration 5.

🌀 Bend and shape petals into suitable form and shape.

🌀 If longer stems are needed, cut desired length of #16 gauge wire, lay alongside twisted petal wires and attach with masking tape.

🌀 Wrap entire stem with floral tape.

Illustration 5

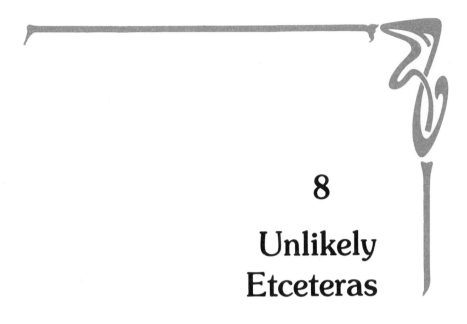

8

Unlikely
Etceteras

What would you think about a flower arrangement made from a cup of lima beans, a roll of aluminum foil, a batch of bread dough, a few grocery sacks and some discarded food cartons? What would you think if the conglomerate turned out to be truly dazzling? Look at Color Plate 13. Such assorted kitchen wares are the ingredients for the flowers.

The epigrammatist who coined the phrase, "Necessity is the mother of invention," surely understood motivation and creativity. A need for something, and especially a need for something unavailable or unaffordable, almost always produces a drive, a force within us, to bring it about. The same is true in the fashioning of flowers. Most of us need some reason to be creative. We want pleasing effects, but we do not always have the means to bring them about. So, we make "silk purses out of sow's ears."

A flower can be made of just about anything. All it takes is your own inventive spirit. The "unspecified additional things," which is the definition of "etcetera," can be grist for your mill. You simply can use any "etcetera" which will work, as long as it does not "infringe on the rights of other's 'etcetera,' etc."

One of the most successful etcetera flowers is the aluminum foil rose, shown in Color Plate 12. There is a story behind it.

The need for such a flower came when we had in our town an important

Happiness is the art of making a bouquet of those flowers within reach.
QUOTED BY BOB GODDARD, ST. LOUIS GLOBE-DEMOCRAT

political function. While it was politically important, the budget for decorating a mammoth civic center in which it was staged was some impossibly low figure like $84! Now you really can't do much in decorating a mammoth civic center for "something like $84."

A few years before, I had designed an aluminum foil rose. When this particular crisis arose, a friend who was chairman of the political happening remembered the rose. She recognized its potential for making an elegant affair in spite of the minimum budget. She had her committee make several hundred roses, each looking for all the world like sterling silver. These were arranged in combination with fresh white mums in inexpensive "silver" containers.

The flowers were centerpieces, placed on tables laid with navy blue velveteen cloths made from "seconds" purchased for a song at a local fabric store. White candles were then placed on each table. The effect was stunning! Since then, the roses have been used for many occasions in our community, inexpensively and handsomely.

Favorite etcetera flowers are some I made several years ago from clear plastic lids. The lids were the type without printing, the sort which come on cartons of cottage cheese or on containers from the delicatessen. First I cut the rims off them. Then I fringed some, scalloped some, put them in layers graduated in size on wire stems with an iridescent glass bead glued to the end of each for a stamen. Leaves were also fashioned of clear plastic. Viva! Here were delicate "crystal" flowers, the only plastic flowers I have ever owned which have been entirely acceptable. They are still in use, arranged casually in a pretty crystal bowl with a little dried baby's breath. Occasionally I tote them to the kitchen sink for a bath under the faucet, replace them in the bowl and continue to enjoy them. While in the midst of making these particular

flowers we ate a lot of packaged foods. My husband wondered aloud which came first, the flowers or the cartons. Were the cartons bought because of the flowers or were the flowers just to use up the cartons?

Once I made some lovely "ceramic" marigolds by gluing ruffled noodles onto a styrofoam ball, painting them with acrylic paints, then spraying them with high gloss clear varnish. I do not recall what my "need" was for those, but they served the purpose and I eventually gave them to someone who admired them.

I must not mislead you, however. Another book could be written some day on all my etceteras which *didn't* work. But the following are some that did. First are flowers for an arrangement — the aluminum foil rose, the tiger lily, the coppertone asters and the white bean flowers. Then I will give you directions for the tooling foil poppy and for the wood veneer zinnias.

Aluminum Foil Rose

Color Plate 12

YOU WILL NEED:

Heavy-duty aluminum foil
Regular aluminum foil
 # 16 gauge stem wire
Masking tape

Black floral tape

ADDITIONAL MATERIALS FOR LEAVES AND CALYXES:

Extra heavy-duty aluminum foil
Quick-sticking white glue
 # 22 gauge wire

Step-by-step for making the rose:

❀ Trace patterns, transfer to carboard and cut out. Label each.

1. MAKE THE FLOWER PARTS.

❀ To make center and buds, make a small hook on one end of # 16 gauge stem wire, then cut a piece of regular foil 6″ by 12″. Lightly fold in half lengthwise but do not crease.

❀ Hold end of folded strip between the thumb and index finger of your left hand; with your right hand wrap it loosely around your thumb and finger to form a roll. Pinch the bottom together. See illustration 1.

❀ Pull hooked stem wire down through center of bud, catching hook inside. Secure with masking tape at base of rolled center. See illustration 2.

❀ To cut petals, tear off two sheets of heavy duty aluminum foil about 10″ by 18″. Place them together back to back so that the shiny sides are to the outside.

❀ Place pattern on the double foil and draw it seven times to make seven petals of double thickness, shiny on both sides.

❀ With a pencil, roll the upper curved edge of each petal to the indentation. See illustration 3.

2. MAKE THE LEAVES.

❀ Make three small leaves and two large leaves for each rose.

❀ Cut # 22 gauge wire into 4½″ lengths.

❀ Cut two squares of extra heavy-duty foil ½″ larger all around than leaf pattern.

A memo to Flower Fashioners. Instructions for sizing fabrics, page 28. Instructions for covering wire, page 31. Bread dough recipe, page 31.

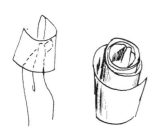

Illustration 1

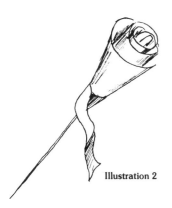

Illustration 2

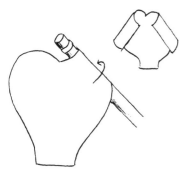

Illustration 3

✿ For large leaf, coat 3″ (2″ for small leaf) of wire with glue and sandwich between the two foil squares placed with dull sides together, leaving the uncoated portion of wire extended at base for attaching to stem. Press together and allow to dry. See illustration 4.

✿ Position pattern on foil square so that wire is in center and cut out. See illustration 5.

✿ Notch sides of leaf as indicated on pattern.

✿ With a lead pencil, score veins in leaf as indicated on pattern. See illustration 6.

3. MAKE CALYXES.

✿ Press together two sheets, dull sides together, of extra heavy-duty aluminum foil.

✿ Draw around calyx pattern, cut out. (Cutting will weld the edges of foil together. If they separate slightly, just press back together.)

4. ASSEMBLE THE ROSE.

✿ Gently cup the middle of the petal with your thumbs, then pinch and pleat the petal base and secure to center roll with masking tape. In this way, tape three petals around the center roll with rolled edge facing *inward*. See illustration 7.

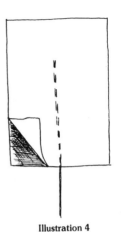

Illustration 4

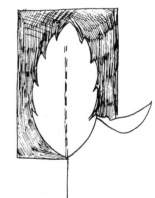

Illustration 5

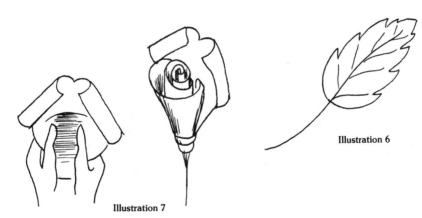

Illustration 7

Illustration 6

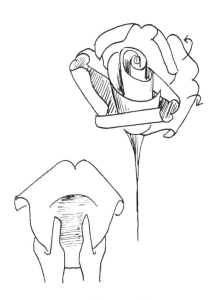

Now tape a final layer of four petals around the rose with the rolled edges facing *outward*. See illustration 8.

Cut a cross in the center of the calyx as indicated on pattern, insert stem of rose through opening, slide up on stem and position around base of rose. Tape in place.

Wrap entire stem with floral tape, attaching three small leaves near top of stem, one or two large leaves lower on the stem. See illustration 9.

Illustration 8

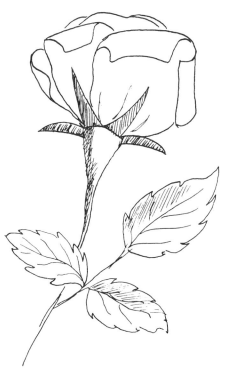

Illustration 9

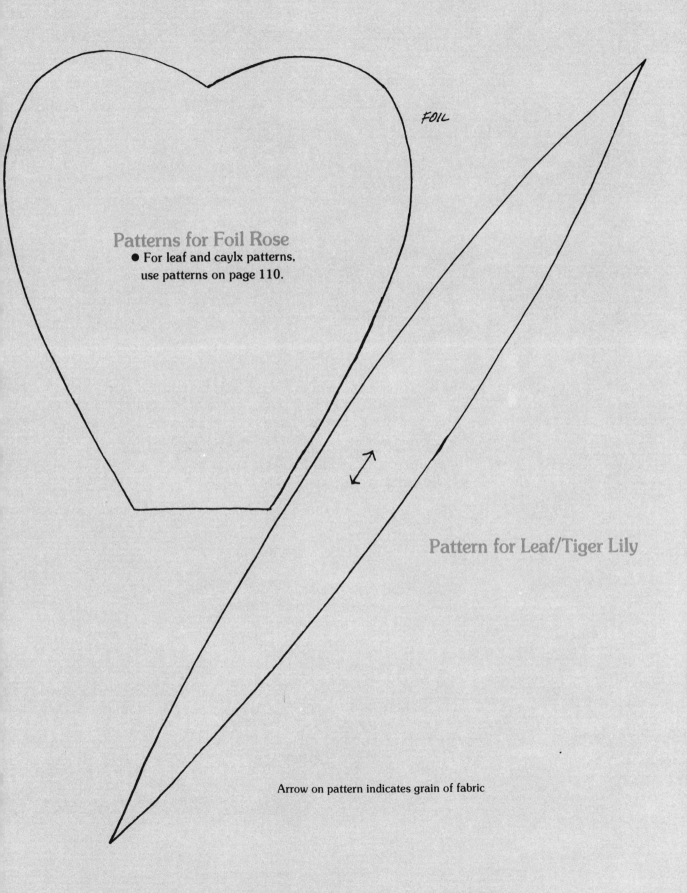

FOIL

Patterns for Foil Rose
● For leaf and caylx patterns,
use patterns on page 110.

Pattern for Leaf/Tiger Lily

Arrow on pattern indicates grain of fabric

Tiger Lilies

Color Plate 12

YOU WILL NEED:

Brown paper bags or parcel wrap

Vinyl wallpaper paste

Half pint can of high-gloss polyurethane varnish

Gold metallic bronzing powder

Bread dough for stamens (See recipe, page 31.)

Small paint brush

Brown and black felt-tip markers

#26 gauge white covered wire for stamens

#22 gauge wire for petals

#16 gauge wire for stems

Masking tape

Black floral tape

ADDITIONAL MATERIALS FOR LEAVES:

Dark brown velveteen

Regular white glue

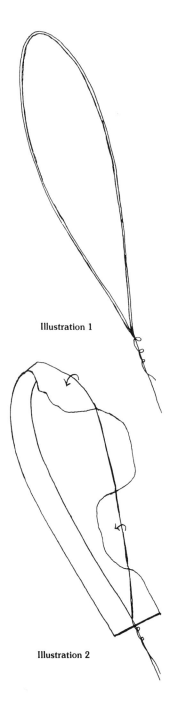

Illustration 1

Illustration 2

Step-by-step for making a tiger lily:

1. MAKE THE PETALS.

🌼 Twist #22 gauge wire into petal shapes, leaving 3″ for the stem. See illustration 1. Make six petals for each flower.

🌼 Using wire petal frames as a guide, cut brown paper into petal shapes. Add about 1″ all around for overlap.

🌼 Mix paste according to package directions, diluting to the consistency of heavy cream. (Paste will thicken with time. Add water if necessary.)

🌼 Soak paper petals in the paste until they are pliable, then mold each around a wire petal, smoothing the overlap to the underside, eliminating all "corners" on the edge of wire. See illustration 2. Lay on edge on a piece of foil to dry overnight.

🌼 Brush two coats of varnish on each petal (allowing to dry between coats). I usually stretch a string across my utility room to hang these on to dry.

🌼 Now add ½ teaspoon of gold bronzing powder to the half pint of varnish. Stir to mix, and brush on each petal. Allow to dry.

To decorate with speckles, loosely twist together stems of six petals and fasten with masking tape. Bend petals down into approximately the shape you want them to be.

With both black and brown felt-tip markers, speckle the petals, heavy near the center base of each petal, graduating to no speckles on the tips of the petals. Use more black speckles near the center. See illustration 3.

Now brush on one more coat of gold varnish which will bleed and soften the speckles slightly. No need to varnish the underside of petals again. Allow to dry. See illustration 4.

2. MAKE STAMENS.

Cut #26 gauge white covered wire into six 5″ pieces for each lily.

Glue to one end of each wire a piece of bread dough the size of a pea. After gluing to the wire, flatten it slightly. Set aside to harden.

3. MAKE THE LEAVES.

Trace and transfer pattern to cardboard and cut out. Label it.

Cut strips of black floral tape in half lengthwise and cover #22 gauge wire.

Cut black covered #22 gauge wire into 11″ pieces.

For each leaf, cut a piece of brown velveteen 10″ by 2″.

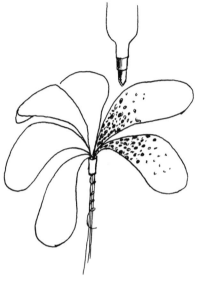

Illustration 3

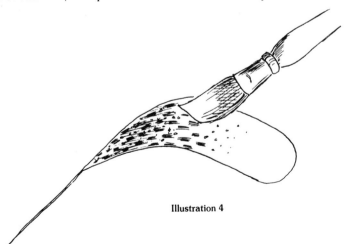

Illustration 4

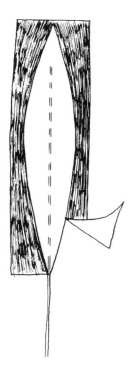

Illustration 5

🌸 Coat 9'' of wire with glue and attach to center back of velveteen, leaving uncoated wire extended at base. Allow to dry. See illustration 5.

🌸 Center leaf pattern on wired velveteen and cut out. Shape.

4. ASSEMBLE THE LILY.

🌸 Remove masking tape from the six petals you have speckled. Place six stamens in the center and rearrange the six petals around them. Twist all stem wires together and secure with masking tape. See illustration 6. Cut a piece of #16 gauge stem wire, lay alongside the twisted stems, and attach with masking tape.

🌸 Wrap entire stem with floral tape, attaching two leaves near the bottom of stem. Shape petals. See illustration 6.

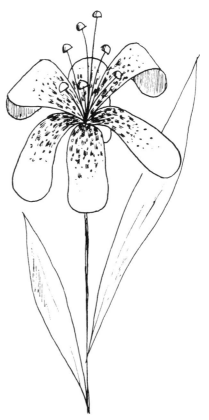

Illustration 6

Coppertone Asters

Color Plate 12

YOU WILL NEED:

Tooling foil or salvaged aluminum food containers such as pie tins or frozen baked goods containers (Tooling foil may be purchased under the brand name Maid-O'Metal or ordered direct from St. Louis Crafts, Box 13033, St. Louis, Mo. 63119.)

Brown and black felt-tip markers (Use deep reddish coppertone or, if you prefer, a lighter golden brown.)

 # 16 gauge wire for stems

Black floral tape

ADDITIONAL MATERIALS FOR LEAVES:

Copper colored velveteen, sized

Quick-sticking white glue

 # 22 gauge black (or brown) covered wire

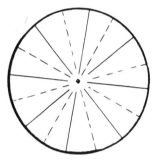

Illustration 1

Step-by-step for making the aster:

Trace and transfer patterns to cardboard and cut out. Label each.

1. MAKE THE FLOWER PARTS.

From pieces of salvaged aluminum or tooling foil, cut one large and one small circle for each flower.

To color flowers, paint an area about the size of a quarter in the center of each circle with black felt tip marker, then color the remainder of the circle with brown marker.

With scissors, clip both circles into pinwheels. See illustration 1.

Cut # 16 gauge stem wire into desired lengths.

Illustration 2

Make a small hook on one end of each stem wire. Wind several layers of black floral tape around the hook, rolling and shaping it into a small ball to serve as a stamen/stem. See illustration 2.

2. MAKE THE LEAVES.

From sized copper velveteen, cut two or three leaves for each flower.

On the back side of each leaf, score veins according to directions on pattern. See illustration 3.

Illustration 3

157

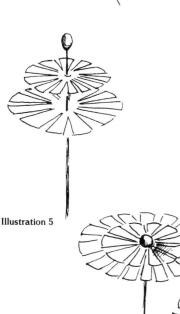

Illustration 4

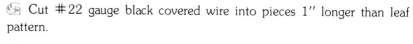
Cut #22 gauge black covered wire into pieces 1″ longer than leaf pattern.

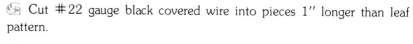
Coat three-fourths of the wire with quick-sticking glue and attach to back of each leaf, leaving the uncoated portion extended at base for attaching to stem. See illustration 4.

3. ASSEMBLE THE ASTER.

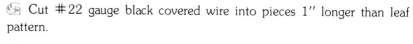
Punch a small hole in the center of each pinwheel. Insert the stem wire into the hole of first the small pinwheel, then the larger one. See illustration 5. Bring both pinwheels up on the stem and position beneath the taped hook.

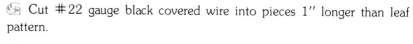
Wind two or three inches of floral tape around the stem wire just beneath the pinwheels, pushing it up on the stem as far as possible to tighten the flower head on the stem. See illustration 6.

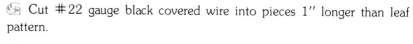
Wrap entire stem with floral tape, attaching two or three leaves as you wrap. Shape flowers according to illustration 7.

Illustration 5

Illustration 6

Illustration 7

Patterns for Asters

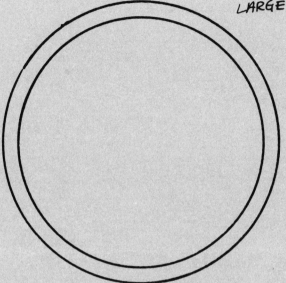

LARGE FLOWER

CUT 1 LARGE CIRCLE
& 1 MEDIUM CIRCLE

SMALL FLOWER

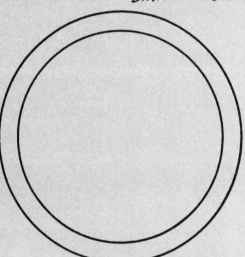

CUT 1 MEDIUM CIRCLE
& 1 SMALL CIRCLE

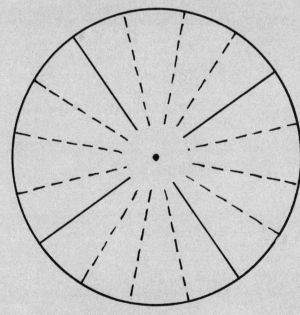

CUT to within 1/2"
OF CENTER.

Arrow on pattern indicates grain of fabric

White Bean Flower

Color Plate 12

YOU WILL NEED:
Dried lima beans

Bread dough for stamens (See recipe, page 31.)

Black felt-tip marker

Regular white glue

#24 gauge wire for petals

#20 gauge wire for stems

Masking tape

Black floral tape

ADDITIONAL MATERIAL FOR LEAVES:

Black duplex crepe paper or black construction paper

Illustration 1

Illustration 2

Illustration 3

Step-by-step for making the bean flower:

1. MAKE THE FLOWER PARTS.

To make stamens, cut #20 gauge wire into suitable stem lengths. To the end of each wire, glue a small pea-sized ball of bread dough. Allow to harden, then color with black felt-tip marker.

To make petals, soak beans in water overnight. (To give you some idea of how many to soak, allowing for some discards you will need about five beans for each flower.)

Remove skins from soaked beans and separate each bean into two halves.

Cut #24 gauge wire into pieces about 2″ long. Insert one end of wire into each bean half while still soft. See illustration 1.

With a small brush, coat each wired bean with glue and allow to dry.

2. ASSEMBLE THE BEAN FLOWER.

Place five wired beans around stamen/stem wire, twist wires of petals around stem and attach with a small piece of masking tape. See illustration 2.

Wrap entire stem with black floral tape, attaching two or three "leaves" made by cutting very thin strips of black crepe paper (cut with the grain) or black construction paper. After leaves are attached, curl the leaves by carefully pulling the blade of scissors along the strip. See illustration 3.

Tooling Foil Poppy

Color Plate 13 (As seen in Family Circle Magazine)

YOU WILL NEED:

Tooling foil for petals and leaves (A roll 15' by 12" wide is enough for 18 single and six double poppies and for 32 leaves. Tooling foil may be purchased under the brand name Maid-O'Metal or ordered direct from St. Louis Crafts, Box 13033, St. Louis, Mo. 63119.)

Regular weight aluminum foil for centers

Matte-finish spray paint in olive green for leaves

Matte-finish spray paint in black for center

High-gloss spray enamel in shades of red, pink, and orange

Clear spray varnish

Green floral tape

Quick-sticking white glue

#16 gauge stem wire

Step-by-step for making the poppy:

Trace and transfer patterns to cardboard and cut out. Label each.

1. MAKE THE FLOWER PARTS.

To prepare center and stem, cut a desired length of #16 gauge stem wire. Make a small hook on one end of wire, coat the hook with glue, then roll around the hook a piece of aluminum foil into a firm ball about 1" in diameter. Dry thoroughly. See illustration 1.

Spray ball with black paint.

For each large double-layer poppy, you will need one 6" diameter circle and one 5" diameter circle for petals and one 3" diameter circle for black center section.

Illustration 1

For each single-layer poppy, you will need one 5" diameter circle for petals and one 3" diameter circle for black center section.

Trace around petal patterns onto tooling foil and cut as many pieces as desired.

With scissors, fringe all the 3" circles to within ½" of center by making slits ⅛" apart. See illustration 2.

Place fringed 3" circles on a layer of newspaper. Spray one side with black paint. Dry thoroughly and spray other side.

Illustration 2

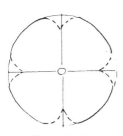

Illustration 3

🖎 Divide the remaining 5″ and 6″ circles into four petals each by cutting into quarters within ½″ of the center. Do not cut through. See illustration 3.

🖎 Trim edges to petal shape as shown in illustration 3.

🖎 With your fingers or with the pliers, flute the petal edges as you would a pie crust.

🖎 Spread circles out on layers of newspaper and spray one side with two coats of red or orange or pink high-gloss enamel, allowing each application to dry thoroughly, preferably overnight.

🖎 Apply one coat of clear varnish and dry. Turn circles over and repeat process on other side.

🖎 After petals are dry, bend gently upward into cup shape.

🖎 Punch a hole in the center of each petal "cup" and each black circle.

2. MAKE THE LEAVES.

🖎 Cut two leaves for each double poppy, one for each single poppy.

🖎 Place cut leaves on a padding of newspaper. Press vein lines into foil with a blunt pencil. See illustration 4.

🖎 Spray each side twice with matte olive green paint; dry after each application.

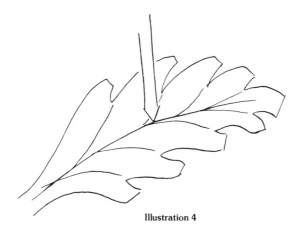

Illustration 4

3. ASSEMBLE THE POPPY.

Insert stem to which painted foil ball is attached, through the hole in one 3″ black center section. Add one 5″ and one 6″ petal cup for the larger blossoms and one 5″ for the smaller one. See illustration 5.

Wrap a piece of floral tape around the stem, pressing it up against the bottom of the cup until the flower feels secure.

With floral tape, wrap remaining stem, attaching the leaves by pressing the stem of leaf around stem of flowers, then wrapping with the tape. See illustration 6.

Bend petals again to improve the cupped effect.

Illustration 5

Illustration 6

163

Veneer Zinnia

Color Plate 14 (As seen in Family Circle Magazine)

YOU WILL NEED:

Wood veneer, birch and/or oak for petals, mahogany and/or walnut for leaves (Veneer comes in small rolls 2″ wide or in rolled sheets of varying size and is available at most lumber and building supply stores. Petals for each of the flowers require 15″ of 2″ wide veneer.)

1″ styrofoam balls

Orange shellac

Brown felt-tip marker

Fabric dyes in orange, pink, yellow, and olive green

Single-edge razor blade

1″ varnish brush for shellac (Brush may be cleaned with household ammonia or denatured alcohol.)

 # 16 gauge stem wire

Brown floral tape

Step-by-step for making a zinnia:

1. PREPARE THE VENEER.

Illustration 1.

Cut birch and/or oak veneer into 2″ by 6″ strips.

With hot tap water, mix about two tablespoons of each color dye in shallow oblong containers. Dip veneer strips into hot water first, then immerse in the dye solution. I dyed some pink, some yellow, some orange. Then I added a little olive green to the yellow as a variation.

Illustration 2

Evenness of color is obtained by rolling the veneer strips, which tend to curl when wet, until color is consistent. Intensity of color depends upon how long the veneer is left in the dye.

Blot the strips with paper towels to remove excess moisture. Then lay flat on newspaper and weight with a plate or saucers to keep flat as possible as they dry.

Illustration 3

2. MAKE THE PETALS.

For each flower, you will need 32 pieces, each ½″ by 1½″. You may get these from two 2″ by 6″ dyed strips cut into 16 pieces each.

Trim each piece as shown, saving all those little corner bits to use as the tight center "petals stamens" in the zinnias. See illustration 1.

3. ASSEMBLE THE ZINNIAS.

With the brown felt-tip marker, color the styrofoam ball.

For the first (the bottom) row of petals, about ¾" of the way down the ball, make a row of nine slits with a razor blade just wide and deep enough so the petals slip in easily.

Dip the base of each petal in glue and insert into the slits at a slight downward angle. See illustration 2.

Add three more rows of slits spaced about $1/16$" apart above the first row (eight, eight, and seven slits respectively). See illustration 3.

Add petals as above.

With scissors, snip off the tips of each row of petals, making the fourth row a little shorter than the third row and the third a little shorter than the second row, etc. See illustration 4.

Dip the sharp tip of the cut-off corner slivers into glue and insert in the center of the flower, placing a few yellow slivers innermost in each flower.

Touch only the edges of each petal with the brown felt-tip marker.

Cut #16 gauge stem wire into desired lengths. Dip the tip of each stem wire into glue and insert in the ball under the flower head. Let glue dry. See illustration 5.

4. MAKE THE LEAVES.

From mahogany or walnut veneer, cut 2" by 8" strips.

Brush both sides with orange shellac to bring out the grain and color of the wood. Let dry.

Trace actual-size leaf pattern on paper, then using the pattern as a guide, cut leaves from veneer strips, one or two for each flower.

Punch a hole in the base of each leaf and thread onto the stem a few inches below the blossom. See illustrations 5 and 6.

Place a dab of glue under each leaf to keep it from slipping.

Wrap stem with floral tape.

Illustration 4

Illustration 5

Illustration 6

Patterns for Poppy

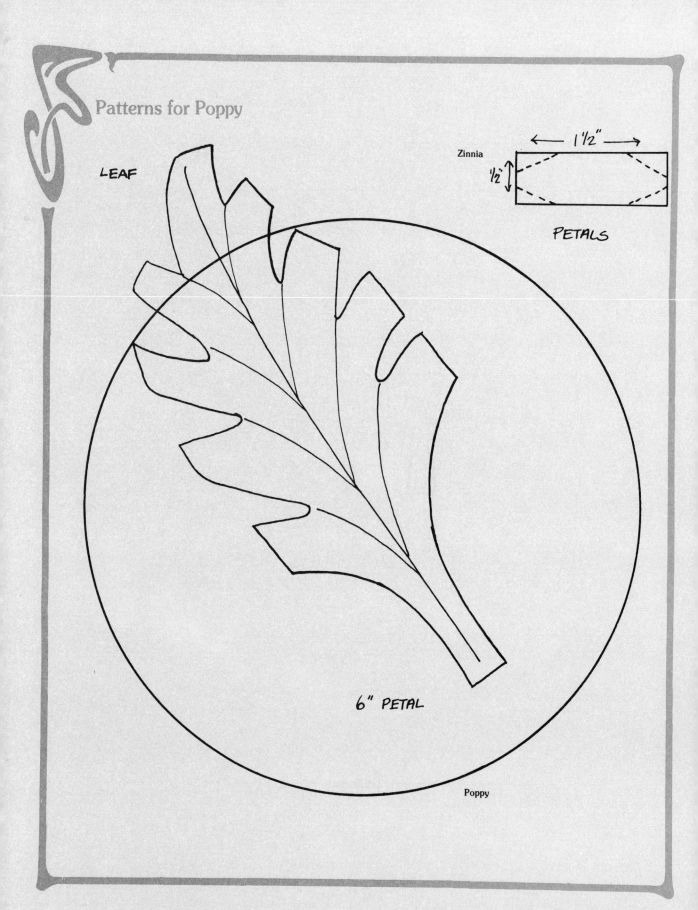

LEAF

Zinnia

1 1/2"

1/2"

PETALS

6" PETAL

Poppy

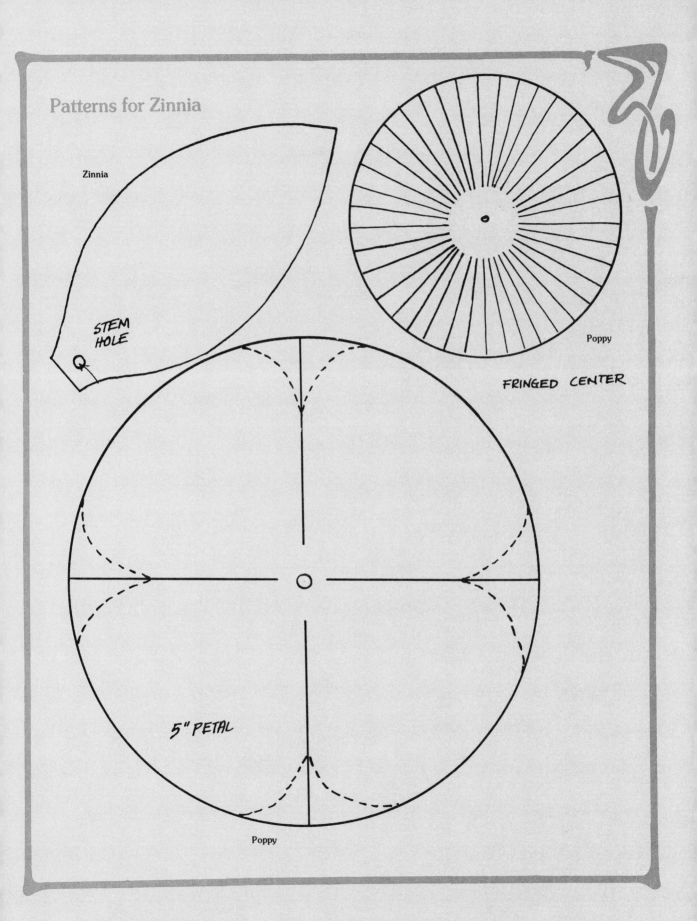

Patterns for Zinnia

Zinnia

STEM
HOLE

FRINGED CENTER

Poppy

5" PETAL

Poppy

JAN/WALKER

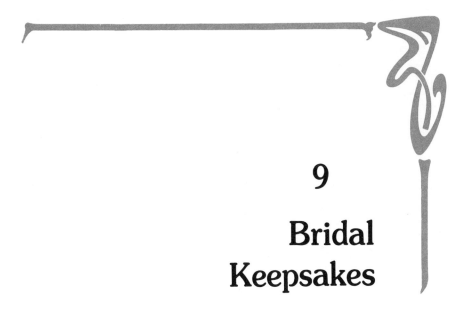

9

Bridal Keepsakes

"Handmade" is fashionable—but "handmade" has always been in vogue. That which we craft ourselves, that into which we put our own ideas, energy, inspiration—love, if you please—is something to cherish.

So it has been since our civilization began. The tiny cradle which great-grandfather hewed from trees he felled, the Revere bowl which may or may not have known the hand of old Paul himself, the crocheted forget-me-not or the satin rose made from an old *Butterick Design for Embroidery*, these are now without price. The crystalized flower some ancestor did from an 1870 *Godey's* is a collector's item. (To crystalize, you "dissolve 18 ounces of burnt alum in a quart of soft spring water . . . Suspend the flower which is to be crystalized, by twine, from a lath for 24 hours . . ." Presto! It is crystalized!)

We are not about to turn our back on the concepts which technology has produced, those which make life more comfortable and pleasant. We will not trade our built-ins for the old-time "safe" which once graced our kitchen. We'll keep the ice maker, the microwave oven and the air-conditioning we now have. They save labor. They give us more time—and this is a paradox—time to devote to hand-doing crafts from which technology has saved us.

Today's young people offer us a clue on this as on other matters. They want the "new" but with it they turn more and more to the "old." They want a new auto—which they can tear apart and make better. They let the kitchen run itself while they try their skill at embroidery, at silk screening, at pottery,

. . . and to hold from this day forward, for better, for worse, for richer, for poorer, in sickness and in health . . .

BOOK OF COMMON PRAYER

at jewelry making. They are environmentalists, wanting to save our resources. They want to do it themselves. I believe our youngsters are directing our thoughts back to a simpler time, back to an era when people cared more about other people, back to the spirit of thoughtfulness and love.

What more appropriate time to express our love for youth than when their "big moment" comes? What other moment is greater than their wedding day? You may not be able to fashion your daughter's wedding dress. That may be beyond your talents as a seamstress. But you can do flowers for her, beautiful flowers made of the finest fabrics. Make them, if not for a daughter, then for a friend, for a niece, for a godchild or for someone you care for very much. And while she may not voice her thoughts in your rhetoric, any blue-jeaned young lady approaching her marriage will surely appreciate your effort. Be sure, however, that it is what *she* wants for her wedding, not what *you* want for her.

Your flowers will give her wedding a special meaning. They offer the advantage of permanence, particularly if you present with the bride's bouquet a glass dome which will encase your gift, making it something "to have and to hold from this day forward." Hand-fashioned flowers may be the only flowers available if you live in a remote area. If you do the wedding flowers yourself, there is no limit on colors; and today's youth are certainly not bound by tradition. If you are thrifty, the flowers you make can represent a monetary savings. Use the rest of the flower budget for lavish live greenery to show your creations to their best advantage. If there is money left, why not invest it in a special piece of furniture for the young couple to use as they begin their life together? Beyond these advantages, the flowers you make will demonstrate your own love, your own devotion. They are true keepsakes, mementos of happy memories.

To stimulate your creative thinking toward the particular wedding in which you are interested, I am giving patterns for one popular choice for brides — roses and their buds, and with it a tiny lily. There is a bridal bouquet made from these. Roses also form the bouquet for the bridesmaids. But consider these only as a beginning for your project. Look through this book. There are ideas waiting to be put to such a grand occasion. Suppose your bride plans a holiday wedding. I can imagine an unusually lovely affair using as your theme the red velvet poinsettia combined with white. Perhaps your bride likes daisies. Consider the daisy pattern made not of paper, as in Chapter 3, but of a silky white polyester, one with a lot of body to it. Or, consider the white silk lilies, big ones and little ones, laced with cascades of white petunias made from accordion pleated ruffled trim with soft green organza leaves and plenty of sprengeri fern. Hybrid tea roses might be the choice. You be the designer. If you do not find the flower pattern you want, invent some of your own.

Unless you chance to live beyond the reach of a florist, it is doubtful you would ever want to dispense with fresh flowers for a wedding. The aroma of garden-fresh roses or gardenias simply goes with a wedding. They fit together. But the suggestion here is that you combine fresh and silk flowers, that you design a bouquet which will have fresh flowers for fragrance and fashioned flowers for memories.

The uses you make of fashioned flowers is determined by the wedding itself. The possibilities are unlimited. Put your flowers with swags and tiers of live leaves, ferns and other greenery to give them a proper background. You might want pew markers, a delightful use of small roses. The altar area is there for you to decorate and so is the reception hall. Design flowers to top your cake. (A bit of plastic under the flowers will protect them and the cake.) Add rosebuds and greenery to the base.

If your wedding is one with a small guest list, another idea is to offer a keepsake for all who attend the event. A rosebud, with its center open, can hold rice or fresh petals or simply be a remembrance. Arrange the buds as a topiary tree. Keepsakes are to be kept and these will last a lot longer than a piece of wedding cake.

White Taffeta Floribunda Rose

Color Plate 15

A memo to Flower Fashioners. Instructions for sizing fabrics, page 28. Directions for covering wire, page 31. Bread dough recipe, page 31.

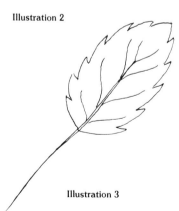

Illustration 1

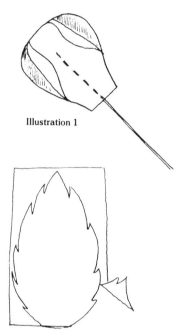

Illustration 2

Illustration 3

YOU WILL NEED:

Fine woven white taffeta, sized (Use one similar to peau de'soie, a lovely silk fabric, if it is available to you.)

Quick-sticking white glue

 # 26 gauge white covered wire

 # 22 gauge wire to lengthen stems

Masking tape

Green floral tape

ADDITIONAL MATERIALS FOR LEAVES:

Avocado green satin floral ribbon, sized

 # 26 gauge green covered wire

Step-by-step for making a floribunda rose:

Trace and transfer pattern to cardboard and cut out. Label each.

1. MAKE THE PETALS.

Cutting two pieces for each petal, each rose will require 14 large petals cut to make seven finished double petals, 12 medium-sized petals cut to make six finished petals, and 12 small petals to make six finished petals.

Stretch edge of petals to ripple.

Cut # 26 gauge white covered wire into pieces 3″ long.

To make each double petal, coat 1″ of wire with glue and sandwich between two petals placed back to back, leaving uncoated end of wire extended at base of petal for assembling. Allow to dry. See illustration 1.

2. MAKE THE LEAVES.

Make three leaves for each flower. (For a bridal bouquet you may not need to have leaves on each flower, but you should have plenty on hand.)

Cut leaves from sized green floral ribbon.

Notch leaves according to pattern illustration. See illustration 2.

Stretch edges to ripple and shape.

Cut # 26 gauge green covered wire into pieces 3½″ long.

To the center back of each leaf, glue a wire, leaving about 1½″ extended at base for attaching to rose. Allow to dry. See illustration 3.

Patterns for Taffeta Floribunda Rose and Organza and Silk Organza Rose

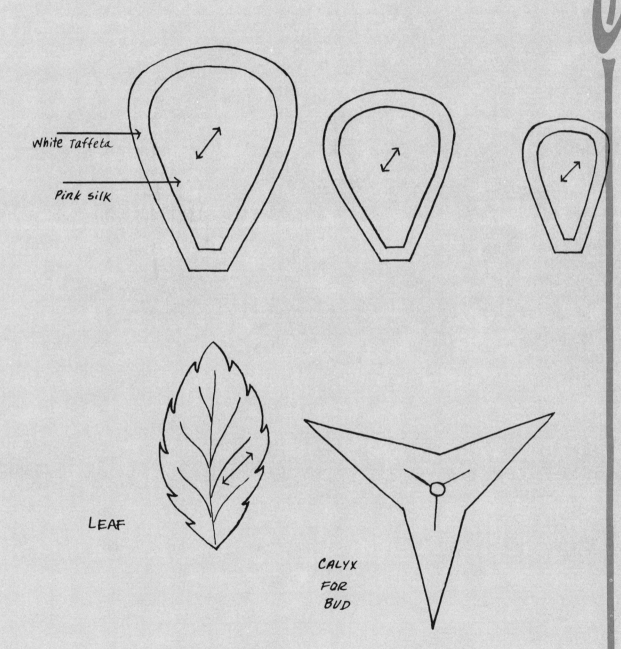

White Taffeta

Pink Silk

LEAF

CALYX
FOR
BUD

Arrow on pattern indicates grain of fabric

3. ASSEMBLE THE FLORIBUNDA ROSE.

🌹 Twist together, facing each other, the six small double petals, then arrange around these the six medium petals evenly spaced. Secure with a thin strip of masking tape to hold together, then add the seven large petals around the outside. See illustration 4. Secure with masking tape.

🌹 Cut a desired length of #22 gauge wire, lay alongside the twisted petal stems and secure with masking tape.

🌹 Wrap stem with floral tape. Attach leaves as you wrap. See illustration 5.

🌹 If necessary, further shape the petal by rolling backward the edge of each single petal with a damp toothpick. See illustration 6.

🌹 Because in a bridal bouquet the calyx of the rose will not show, it is not included here. However, if you would like to use these flowers in other ways, it is suggested you use the calyx pattern and instructions given for the yellow organdy roses on page 110 and 111.

Illustration 4

Illustration 5

Illustration 6

The White and Pink Organdy and Silk Organza Rose

Color Plate 15

Also included in the bridal bouquet is the white and pink organdy and silk organza rose. The same materials and step-by-step should be used as for the taffeta rose with the following exceptions.

SUBSTITUTE THESE MATERIALS FOR THE WHITE TAFFETA:

White organdy, sized *Pale pink (or peach) organza, sized*
White silk organza, sized

SUBSTITUTE THESE STEPS:

🌸 Reduce size of pattern by ⅛″.

🌸 For each of the six small petals, cut one piece of white organdy and one piece of pink (or peach) silk organza.

🌸 Sandwich glue-coated wire between the two pieces for a double petal.

🌸 For each of the rest of the petals, put together with glue-coated wire one organdy petal and one silk petal.

🌸 Assemble by arranging pink (or peach) and white small petals in center with all large white petals arranged around them.

Pink and Peach Floribunda Rose

Color Plate 15

The floribunda rose used in the bridesmaid's bouquet is made the same as the white taffeta floribunda rose with the following exceptions.

SUBSTITUTE THESE MATERIALS IN PLACE OF WHITE TAFFETA:

One shade pink organdy (or peach), two shades of slightly darker pink (or peach) silk organza *#26 gauge white covered wire dipped very briefly in coral dye (Use in supporting petals of both pink and peach roses.)*

SUBSTITUTE THESE STEPS:

🌸 Reduce pattern size by ⅛″

🌸 For each of the six small petals, cut one piece of darkest pink silk organza and one piece of pink organdy. Sandwich the glue-coated wire between the two pieces for a double petal.

🌸 Make each of the rest of the petals with one piece of the other shade of pink silk organza and one piece of pink organdy.

Chiffon Rosebuds

Color Plate 15

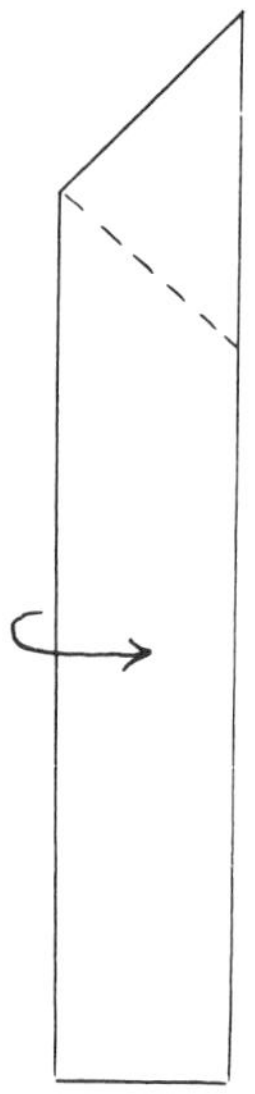

Illustration 1

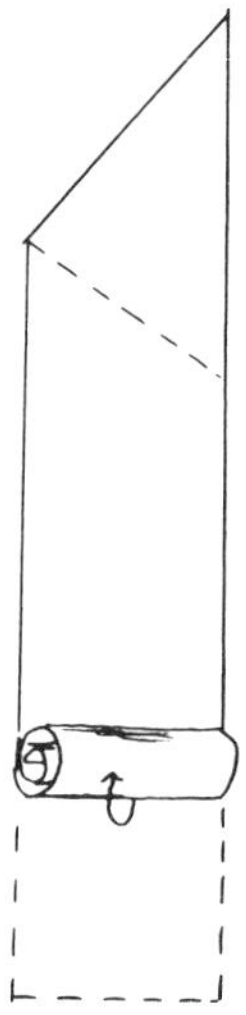

Illustration 2

Illustration 3

Illustration 4

YOU WILL NEED:

Shades of pink and orange chiffon, sized
#22 gauge wire
Medium green cotton for calyxes, sized

Masking tape
Green floral tape

Step-by-step for making a rosebud:

Trace and transfer pattern to cardboard and cut out. Label.

1. MAKE THE ROSEBUD PARTS.

Cut one piece of chosen color of organza for each bud.

Make a small hook on one end of a #22 gauge wire cut 12″ long. (You will cut these stems later to the length necessary for the bouquet.)

Lightly fold in half lengthwise but do not crease the chiffon piece, so that the longer side folds down over the shorter side. See illustration 1.

Hold straight end of folded strip between the thumb and index finger of left hand and with your right hand wrap it loosely around thumb and finger of your left hand to form a roll. See illustration 2.

Insert the hooked wire into top of bud and pull through bud, hooking the wire on fabric inside the bud. See illustration 3.

Pinch base of roll together around wire and secure with the strip of masking tape.

Cut calyx from green cotton. Slit a cross in the center as indicated on pattern.

2. MAKE THE LEAVES AS FOR WHITE TAFFETA ROSE, PAGE 172.

3. ASSEMBLE BUD.

Insert bud stem in center slit of calyx, pull calyx up on stem around base of bud, then wrap the stem with floral tape, attaching three leaves near the top. See illustration 4.

Pattern for Chiffon Rosebud

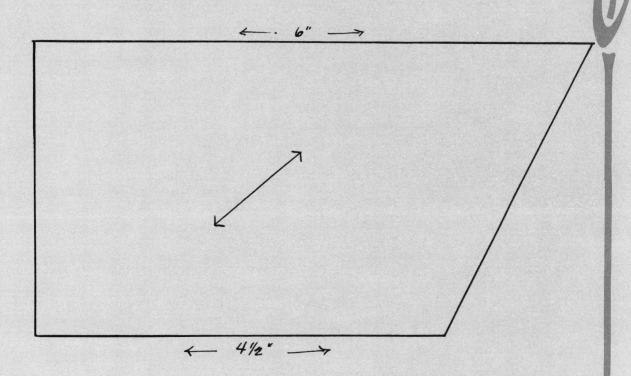

6"

4½"

Pattern for Satin Lily

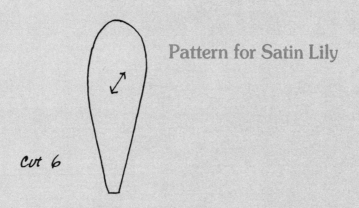

Cut 6

Arrow on pattern indicates grain of fabric

White Satin Lily

Color Plate 15

YOU WILL NEED:

Heavy white satin, sized

 # 26 gauge white covered wire

 # 26 gauge green covered wire for stamens

 # 22 gauge wire for stems

Bread dough (See recipe, page 31.)

Quick-sticking white glue

Masking tape

Green floral tape

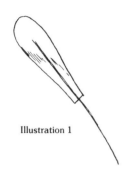

Illustration 1

Step-by-step for making lily:

🐚 Trace and transfer pattern to cardboard and cut out. Label.

1. MAKE THE FLOWER PARTS.

🐚 To make stamens, cut #26 gauge green covered wire into six 2½″ pieces.

🐚 To one end of each stamen wire, glue a tiny ball of bread dough, flattened slightly. Allow to harden.

🐚 Cut six petals for each flower from sized white satin.

🐚 Stretch edge slightly to shape.

🐚 Cut #26 gauge white covered wire into 2½″ pieces.

🐚 Glue a wire to the center back of each petal, leaving 1″ extended at base of petal for assembling. Allow to dry. See illustration 1.

Illustration 2

2. ASSEMBLE THE LILY.

🐚 Arrange the six petals facing each other around the six stamens. Twist all stems together. Secure with a thin strip of masking tape. See illustration 2.

🐚 Cut a 12″ length of #22 gauge wire and lay alongside the twisted petal stems. Wrap stem with green floral tape. See illustration 3.

🐚 Shorten stem as necessary when placing in bouquet.

Illustration 3

The Bridal Bouquet

Color Plate 15

YOU WILL NEED:

About six white taffeta roses

Five organdy and silk roses

About 17 small white satin lilies

Approximately 18 chiffon rosebuds in shades of peach, pink, and apricot.

Step-by-step for assembling the bouquet:

Cut a 1″ slice off a 4″ styrofoam ball. In the center of the flat side, insert one end of a wooden tongue depressor or dowel to serve as a handle. Wrap handle with floral tape.

Cut the stems of the roses to a length of approximately 4″. Insert first into the styrofoam the white taffeta roses, using the Bride's Bouquet illustration as a guideline for placement.

Add the white organdy and silk roses, filling in with rosebuds and lilies according to the illustration.

To give the cascade appearance at base of bouquet, insert long stems of lilies and rosebuds at different levels. Note illustration.

With floral tape, attach a piece of #22 gauge wire to strands of live sprengeri fern. Insert fern strands and intertwine with rosebuds an lilies.

When arrangement is satisfactory, brush glue around those stems of buds, lilies, and ferns inserted at base to effect a cascade. This will insure that they stay intact.

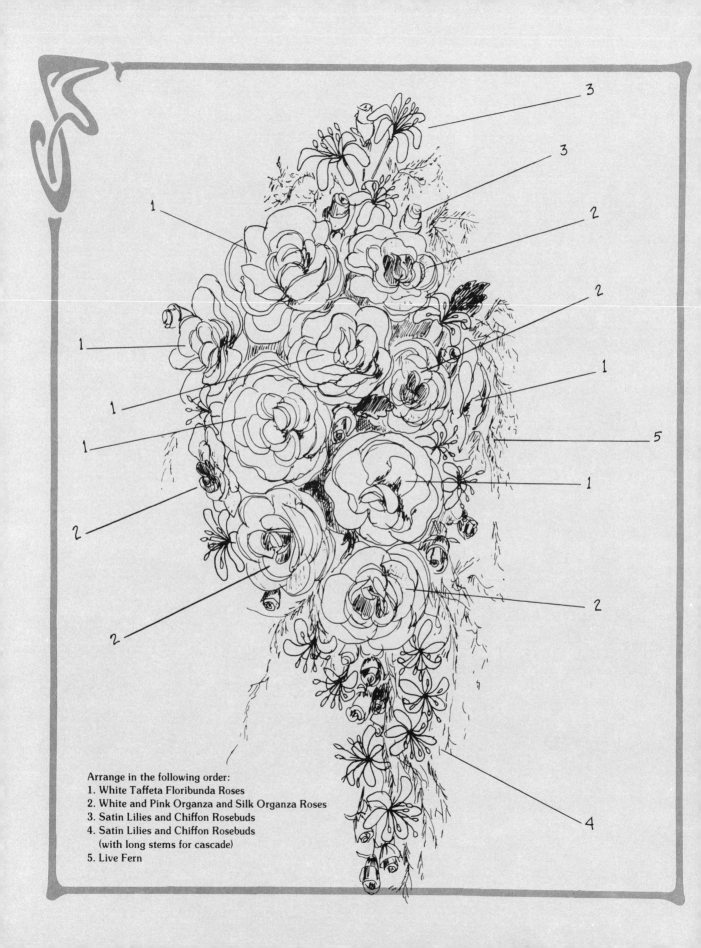

Arrange in the following order:
1. White Taffeta Floribunda Roses
2. White and Pink Organza and Silk Organza Roses
3. Satin Lilies and Chiffon Rosebuds
4. Satin Lilies and Chiffon Rosebuds
   (with long stems for cascade)
5. Live Fern

The Bridesmaid's Bouquet

Color Plate 15

YOU WILL NEED:

Approximately six peach or apricot roses

Five pink roses

About nine white satin lilies

About 13 pink, apricot, and peach rosebuds

❧ Assemble in the same manner as the bridal bouquet, using the colored roses rather than white. Cascade should be shorter than that for the bride's bouquet.

Other uses for bridal fashioned flowers:

❧ As a pew marker, combine rosebuds with fresh greenery

❧ As a nosegay for attendant

❧ As bouquets for the flower girls

❧ As decoration for the top of the bridal cake

❧ As the centerpiece for a reception table

❧ As corsages for the mothers of the bride and the bridegroom

❧ As altar flowers

❧ As a memento for wedding guests (Arrange rosebuds filled with rice on a six″ styrofoam ball to form a topiary tree. Set outside the reception hall where guests can select one as a memento.)

10

Permanent Pot Plants . . . When Yours Won't Bloom

So the pot of violets you bought to decorate the coffee table in your living room is just about shot—before you decide whether it would look better there or out in the foyer. So the geraniums are beginning to lose their petals just when you want them to look their best. So the begonia you have been nursing along has lost its delicate little flowers and you have company coming.

When your pot plants take to their contrary ways, when they just simply will not bloom, shouldn't you have already fashioned your own?

It is a fact that pot plants have come into their own. You are just not anybody unless you are "into" pot plants. A kaleidoscope of color to give splash to a neutral corner, the dramatic emphasis of a bank of hydrangea, the delicate fascination of an intricate caladium, these bid you welcome to our homes. And the hanging baskets! They festoon porches and patios. Magazines, books, pamphlets, newspapers, coach us daily on how to grow whatever it is which flourishes in pots.

This chapter on fashioning your own pot plants is done especially for those of you who find joy in the daily presence of green and growing plants but you simply cannot bring them off. Disease, alas, besets your plants. The life style you have cut out for yourself rules out greenhouses. You try, but yours are a bit scraggly. You give it all you have, but your African violets will not bloom. So why not try these? They are fun to make, a pleasure to show.

You buy some flowers for your table;
You tend them tenderly as you're able;
You fetch them water from hither and thither—
What thanks do you get from it all?
They wither.

HOFFENSTEIN

183

Much has been said of late about the advantages which come when you "talk" with your pot plants. With these plants, you may find yourself doing some talking before you get through. But conversation won't help much once you are finished. I want to show you two versions of the plants. One will stand alone. The other is a blossom you can work into a blossomless plant, one which will fit harmoniously with a flower which just won't bloom. With these varieties, you will be supplied with the color which both you and your home need and no worry about blooming seasons.

In designing the flowers offered here, I have concentrated on accuracy. I tried to make these look like the real thing. Petals appear genuine. Leaves seem lifelike. A pot plant should be like a pot plant. In designing other flowers be imaginative and inventive. Be exotic and daring. But when doing a pot plant, follow nature's rule. Fashion blossoms and leaves as nature made them.

You will notice that a pot plant is a leafy flower, most of the time. Many are nothing but leaves. I am not presenting one of these. If you like leaves, be my guest. Instead, I have designed a geranium, a violet, a blue and white hydrangea. Then I have done a begonia, just the blossom, not the whole plant. You may find these handy tucked in with your hanging begonia—see if anyone can tell the difference.

The leaves I use in all these plants are of primary importance. Whether or not a geranium is blooming, you know it is a geranium because of the construction of each distinctive leaf. You know without prompting that those flowers over there with their rich velvet leaves are violets. Certainly, the hydrangea is . . . well, a hydrangea.

The blossoms for the violet and for the begonia have their own distinct shapes. Not so, the geranium and the hydrangea. One little pattern serves for both flower "heads," the flowerets of both. This same pattern would also make phlox. What distinguishes the geranium, the hydrangea, and the phlox are the colors of their blossoms and the distinctive leaves each has.

Fashioned pot plants make themselves right at home in your house or your apartment from bathroom to patio, from kitchen to entryway. Look through a magazine for ideas on home decor. The rooms have pot plants. So does any attractive display of furniture at a store. Or make a pot plant for somebody's office. The best dressed offices have pot plants. Fashioned plants have special advantages: they require no water nor do they need a light to make them grow. They crave no fertilizer, no insecticide. All they need is a corner to brighten.

A Pot of Geraniums

Color Plate 16

YOU WILL NEED:

Two shades of red cotton sateen, sized (I dyed some old drapery lining which my mother—a frugal woman—had saved. She thought "someone might need that some day." Somebody did.)

Red felt-tip marker

Rubbing alcohol

Small watercolor brush

 # 24 gauge green covered wire

 # 16 gauge wire for stems

Masking tape

Green floral tape

ADDITIONAL MATERIALS FOR LEAVES AND BUDS:

Medium green cotton twill, heavily sized

Olive green dye

Brown felt-tip marker

Quick-sticking white glue

Bread dough (See recipe, page 31.)

A memo to Flower Fashioners. Instructions for sizing fabrics, page 28. Instructions for covering wire, page 31. Bread dough recipe, page 31.

Step-by-step for making a geranium:

Trace and transfer patterns to cardboard and cut out. Label each.

1. MAKE THE FLOWERET.

Each flowerhead will require from 30 to 50 flowerets. Cut three petals for each floweret. (Use two or three shades of red to add depth to each floweret.)

Cut # 24 gauge green covered wire into 8″ pieces.

Bend each wire in half, twisting around center of first petal. Add second petal, twisting once, then add third petal, twisting balance of two strands of wire together. See illustration 1.

With red felt-tip marker, color edges of the six petals and darken the center of the floweret. Then with watercolor brush dipped in alcohol, bleed and blend the colors. See illustration 2.

2. MAKE THE LEAVES.

Make approximately two small, three medium and three or four large leaves for each blossom. It will be good, also, to make five or six leaves to be assembled on a stem without blossoms to add to the "potted" look for your plant.

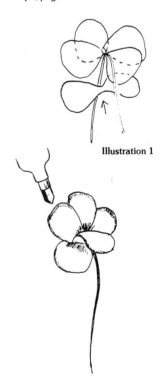

Illustration 1

Illustration 2

185

Illustration 3

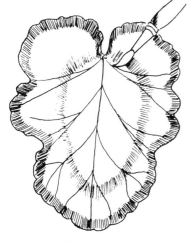

Illustration 4

🐝 Cut the leaves from heavily sized (fairly stiff) green cotton fabric. Pull and stretch the edges to ripple.

🐝 With brown felt-tip marker and watercolor brush dipped in alcohol, make light smudgy markings on the top side of leaf. See illustration 3. With watercolor brush dipped in olive green dye, go over these same markings, darkening the area with green. Also darken the edge of leaf with green dye and paint on veins. See illustration 4. Allow to dry.

🐝 Cut #24 gauge green covered wire into pieces from 4″ to 8″ long.

🐝 With quick-sticking glue, attach a wire to the center back of each leaf, allowing balance of wire to extend beyond the base of leaf for attaching to plant. Allow to dry. See illustration 5.

3. MAKE THE BUDS.

🐝 Each bud should contain three or four flowerets and 12 to 14 "peps" (unopened flowerets).

🐝 To make peps, cut #24 gauge green covered wire into 3″ pieces. To one end of each wire glue a small pea-sized piece of bread dough. Allow to dry, then color it with red felt-tip marker.

🐝 Assemble together flowerets and peps, twisting their stems together and securing with masking tape. Shape the peps as shown in illustration 6.

🐝 Wrap stem with floral tape, attaching two small leaves near top of stem.

4. ASSEMBLE THE GERANIUM.

🐝 Gather together 30 to 50 flowerets. Twist together the bottom 1½″ of their stems and fasten with masking tape.

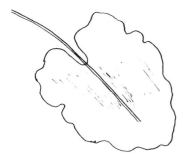

Illustration 5

Illustration 6

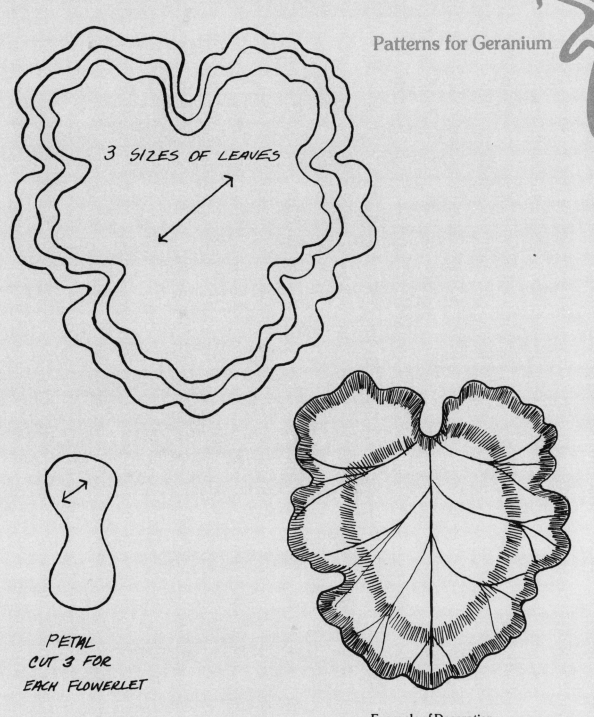

3 SIZES OF LEAVES

PETAL
CUT 3 FOR
EACH FLOWERLET

Example of Decoration

Arrow on pattern indicates grain of fabric

🐚 Cut a desired length of #16 gauge wire, lay alongside the twisted petal stems, and attach with masking tape.

🐚 Wrap entire stem with floral tape, attaching seven to nine leaves and one bud on each stem. Always place the smaller leaves near the top of stem and the larger leaves near the bottom. See illustration 7.

🐚 To make extra leaves to fill in the plant, wrap a desired length of #16 gauge wire with floral tape, attaching five to seven leaves as you wrap.

5. PUT PLANT IN POT.

🐚 Cut styrofoam to fit flower pot, leaving about 2″ at top of pot empty. Attach to pot with floral sticking adhesive, available at floral shops.

🐚 Cover top of styrofoam with potting soil. (Less authentic looking but much neater to keep is a material known as sphagnum moss available at floral and hobby shops.)

🐚 Press stems of blossoms and leaves into the pot. Shape blossoms.

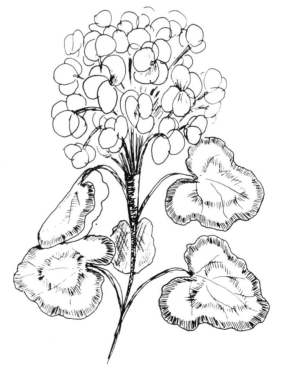

Illustration 7

The Hydrangea Plant

Color Plate 16

YOU WILL NEED:

White medium weight cotton fabric, sized (You may dye fabric light blue, if you prefer, but keep it out of the sun because it will fade.)

Olive green dye (Use to decorate white blossom. To decorate blue blossom, use purple dye and household bleach.)

Watercolor brush

 # 26 gauge green covered wire

 # 16 gauge wire for stems

Masking tape

Green floral tape

ADDITIONAL MATERIALS FOR LEAVES:

Dark green velveteen, sized

Quick-sticking white glue

 # 24 gauge green covered wire

Step-by-step for making hydrangea:

Trace and transfer patterns to cardboard and cut out. Label each.

1. MAKE THE FLOWER PARTS.

Each flower head will require from 60 to 75 flowerets.

Each floweret requires two petals.

Cut petals from white sized cotton (or light blue if you prefer).

To make flowerets, cut #26 gauge green covered wire into 8″ pieces. Bend in center and twist around center of one petal. Add another petal and twist around center to give a four-petal floweret. See illustration 1.

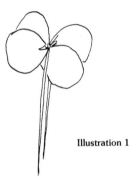

Illustration 1

Twist balance of two strands of wire tightly together making a stem for the floweret.

To decorate, dip watercolor brush in a dab of olive green dye and touch edges of petals as well as the center of petals. See illustration 2. (In making blue flowerets, dip brush in a very weak solution of bleach and water and remove some color from edges of petals and center. You may further decorate edges by dipping brush in a dab of purple dye to color centers and edges of petals.)

Illustration 2

2. MAKE THE LEAVES.

Make 15 to 18 leaves for each blossom and several leaves extra to be put on stems alone and added to potted plant.

Patterns for Hydrangea

Pattern of Scoring

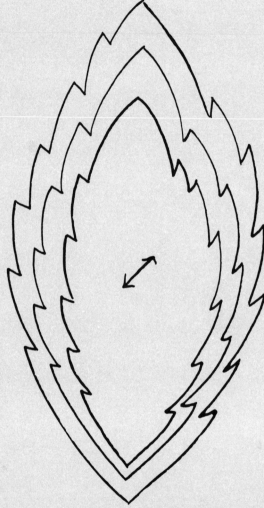

3 SIZES OF LEAVES

PETAL
CUT 2 FOR
each Flowerlet

Arrow on pattern indicates grain of fabric

❧ Cut leaves from sized green velveteen.

Score back of each leaf as indicated on illustration 3.

❧ Cut #24 gauge green covered wire into pieces 6″ to 8″ long.

❧ With quick-sticking glue, attach a wire to the center back of each leaf, leaving the balance of wire extended at base for attaching to stem.

3. ASSEMBLE THE HYDRANGEA.

❧ Gather together 50 to 75 flowerets and twist together the bottom 1½″ of stems and secure with masking tape.

❧ Cut a desired length of #16 gauge wire, lay alongside twisted floweret stems and attach with masking tape.

❧ With floral tape, attach five to seven leaves to one central leaf stem to make a cluster of leaves on a single stem.

❧ Attach two or three of these leaf clusters to stem of flowers as you wrap the entire stem with floral tape. See illustration 4.

Illustration 3

4. PUT PLANT IN POT AS INSTRUCTED ON PAGE 188.

Illustration 4

A Pot of Violets

Color Plate 16 (As seen in Family Circle Magazine*)*

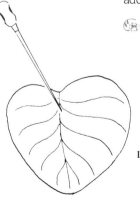

Illustration 1

YOU WILL NEED:

Lavender velveteen, sized

Yellow, green, and purple felt-tip markers

Bread dough (See recipe, page 31.)

 # 22 gauge green covered wire

 # 16 gauge wire for stems

Masking tape

Green floral tape

ADDITIONAL MATERIALS FOR LEAVES:

Green rayon velvet, sized

Quick-sticking white glue

Step-by-step for making a violet:

Trace and transfer patterns to cardboard and cut out. Label each.

1. MAKE THE FLOWER PARTS.

To make stamens, cut # 22 gauge green covered wire into 5" lengths.

Pinch off small pea-sized pieces of bread dough, roll into tiny balls, and glue on one end of each wire. Allow to harden, then paint with yellow marker.

For each bunch of violets, cut about 12 to 15 flowers from the sized lavender velveteen.

To decorate violets, shade with purple marker by lightly stroking the flower from center outward. See illustration 1.

2. MAKE THE LEAVES.

For each bunch of violets, cut from sized green velvet three small leaves, three medium leaves, and three or four large leaves. Make extra leaves to be added singly when potting violets.

Score back of leaves as indicated. See illustration 2.

 Illustration 2

Patterns for Violet

PETALS

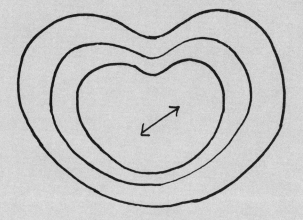

LEAF...
3 SIZES

Arrow on pattern
indicates grain of fabric

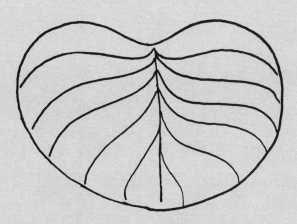

Pattern of Scoring

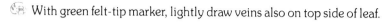

✿ With green felt-tip marker, lightly draw veins also on top side of leaf.

✿ Cut #22 gauge green covered wire into 5″ pieces.

✿ With quick-sticking glue, attach a wire to center back of each leaf. When dry, bend wire at 90° angle at base of leaf before attaching to flower stem. See illustration 3.

3. ASSEMBLE THE VIOLETS.

Illustration 3

✿ Place stems of 12 to 15 violets together. Secure at base of stems with masking tape.

✿ Cut a desired length of #16 gauge wire, lay alongside flower stems and secure with masking tape.

✿ Wrap entire stem with green floral tape, attaching small leaves near top around flower, then the larger leaves lower on the stem. See illustration 4.

4. PUT PLANT IN POT AS INSTRUCTED ON PAGE 188.

Illustration 4

Begonia Blossoms *(or bougainvillea, if you prefer)*

Color Plate 16

YOU WILL NEED:

2″ accordion pleated white ruffling

Needle and thread

Fabric dye: rose, pink, and orange

Red and orange felt-tip markers

Cotton balls

Rubbing alcohol

26 gauge wire

Green floral tape

Step-by-step for making begonia:

1. MAKE THE FLOWERS.

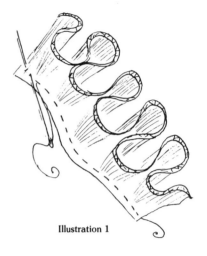

Illustration 1

Dye ruffling pink and orange.

Cut ruffling into 9″ and 7″ pieces. (You don't want them all the same size.)

Trim off binding from bottom of ruffling, then with needle and thread make a running stitch along edge about ¼″ from bottom. See illustration 1.

Draw up tight and tack.

Cut # 26 gauge wire into pieces 5″ to 8″ long.

Make a hook on one end of wire. Insert wire into center of blossom and pull through, catching the hook on fabric inside.

Wrap stem with green floral tape. See illustration 2.

2. DECORATE THE FLOWERS.

To further shade and decorate, paint the edge of pink blossoms with red felt-tip marker, then blend the colors with cotton ball dipped in alcohol.

Do the same on the orange blossom, painting the edge with orange felt-tip marker.

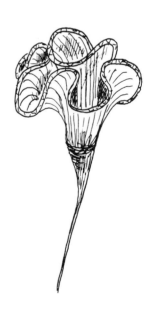

Illustration 2

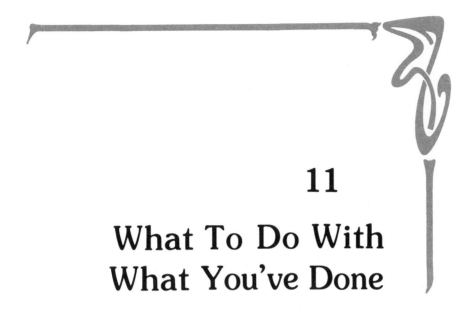

11

What To Do With What You've Done

The great joy of possession is display, showing what you have done or achieved, standing back to await the appreciation for your efforts. This is especially true with flower fashioning—why else, pray tell, would you have put in the time and effort creating such things of beauty? You surely will not hide your handicraft under the well-known bushel.

Flower arranging is an art form in itself, one closely related to painting and to sculpture. In your community library you will find numerous articles and books devoted to teaching you this art—if you do not already know it. So it would be completely unrealistic to suggest that I could instruct you in a few pages, even if I were qualified. Nor is that my intention. I do, however, hope to persuade you to learn by doing. We learn to walk by walking; we learn to dance by dancing; we learn to type by typing. You could read all the books on the shelves about arranging flowers but you will never learn "what to do with what you've done" until you choose a container, put in it something to anchor your flowers, then set your posies in place.

I remember something I read many years ago about the great sculptor Auguste Rodin. When asked once what major principles he used to sculpt so beautifully, he replied, "Oh, it is very simple. You choose a piece of stone, grab a chisel, and chip away everything you don't want." Like Rodin, the experienced flower arranger makes it look easy. But, of course, he too has learned by doing. You also can know as much about it as you want to know, can become as proficient as you are willing to be.

I compare my own efforts at flower arranging to football. I genuinely enjoy a good football game even though I do not know all the rules — nor do I really want to understand the meanings of all those technical terms. But I am sure my enjoyment of the sport is handicapped by what I don't understand. So it is with flower arranging. You may enjoy making the flowers, but when it comes to putting them together in a display, you should at least know when to punt. You may not be interested in winning the championship, but you can at least enjoy the game. The important point is that you "do" because there is no other way in which to learn.

Using a few guidelines and your own instincts, you become acquainted with materials and rules which are, at first, uncomfortable. As you become more familiar with these elements you gradually gain confidence. Unconsciously you begin executing the creative instincts you employed when you made the flowers. You learn by doing. With practice comes skill. Here, again, your first efforts may not be the best. No need to apologize. I wouldn't be at all surprised to learn that Rodin, in his first efforts, "chipped away" some of what he *did* want. With each additional attempt, your innate sense of design will surface as you gain confidence and become free of that rule-bound feeling. You will begin to trust your eye's judgment. It isn't even necessary for you to know why this flower or that one looks better in this or that vase unless you *want* to know.

So here we are in a punting situation. We've fashioned our flowers. Now we need some idea of what to do with what we've done. Fashion in flowers, like fashion in clothing, changes with the times. A more relaxed, informal lifestyle has come into being in recent years. Flower arrangements, I do believe, reflect that same trend. A book by Diane Love, *Flowers Are Fabulous . . . for Decorating*, will help you in this field. It is an excellent source for you on arranging fashioned flowers with style. She covers in detail every facet of the subject — from where to place flowers in your home to which blossoms to place next into the vase. But in case you are anxious merely to get acquainted with this art form, let me give you some basics. These are ideas for you on the container you might use, on the shape of your arrangement, on the "line" and "filler" materials, on the "mechanics" which keep flowers in place.

There is a good chance that when you chose your flowers you had already a notion of where you would like to display them. Your decision on "where" could determine "what" container you should use. Or, perhaps, you selected flowers with a special vase or bowl in mind, did flowers to fit the container, not the other way around. Whatever your reason, your own common sense is the best asset you have when it comes to display.

The container you choose should be compatible in feeling and in mood

Instinct is untaught ability.

BAIN

with the placement of it. (A Little Red Riding Hood basket, you already know, will not look appropriate in the center of a formal dining table.) It is important to coordinate color and texture of the container with the flowers. (Just because your mother-in-law gave you a lovely, delicate opaline vase for Christmas is not reason enough to fill it with, say, sunflowers.) It is necessary to keep the size of the container in proportion to the size of the flowers. (Little short-stemmed pansies in a tall crystal vase? You wouldn't consider it.)

So you see, there is much you know already, know by instinct, about displaying flowers. There are precepts you have not been conscious of until you tried them. I could give you countless do's and don'ts about where to put the flowers, about the flowers best suited to each room, but I am convinced that a sensitive eye is better than the most elaborate rules and techniques. Let me say, just use the good principles of color and scale you employ in dressing, that you apply ingenuity, that you experiment, that you try first the containers you have already.

Flowers are related to all the offices and relations of human life.

GODEY'S LADY'S BOOK

If you are a novice at displaying flowers, you may not as yet have developed this sense of good design, so it will be well to acquaint you with certain fundamental shapes most arrangements take.

The round or oval (see illustration 1) is a pleasing design, the one most commonly used. It repeats the round or circular shape of many flowers and it can be fashioned as "tight" or as "loose" as you want it. The round design looks well from all sides. It has no "blanks." If it appears too monotonous, add some spiky material such as eucalyptus. Lately, I have noticed a trend toward the addition to arrangements of grassy wispy material which is very attractive. Try cutting these grassy wisps from very thin strips (with the grain) from green duplex crepe paper. Attach to a piece of wire and add to your arrangement. An example of the round shape can be seen in Color Plate 12, a mass arrangement of etceteras.

Beauty, like wit, to judges should be shown;
Both most are valued where they best are known.

LYTTLETON

The triangular (see illustration 2) is a symmetrical arrangement of the traditional and the modern style. It can be scaled up or down according to your flowers. It can be broad or narrow, high or low. In following this design,

Illustration 1
Round or Oval

Illustration 2
Triangular

Illustration 3
Crescent

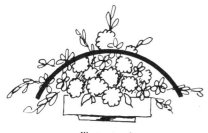

Illustration 4
Convex Curve

Illustration 5
Torch

establish the height and the width, usually with flowers or foliage. Next, establish a focal point of interest, done with larger or darker flowers at the center just above the container's rim. Finally you fill in with flowers of varied stem lengths, grouping colors rather than putting them in at random. The bouquet looks well when viewed from various angles. An example of the triangular shape can be seen in Color Plate 2, the cotton blossoms.

The crescent design (see illustration 3) is more formal in its nature and also requires more skill and experience than do the mass shapes. It is, nonetheless, a satisfying way to arrange fashioned flowers. Blossoms you make give an added advantage: you do not have to worry that the stems will snap just as you are trying to bend them into the design. Fresh flowers will not always allow such manipulation. An example of the crescent design can be seen in Color Plate 1, buttercups and daisies.

The convex curve (see illustration 4) is excellent when you are designing flowers to be used as a centerpiece on a dining table. Guests can see across them. They will not interfere with conversation. The design does not need to be tall. Well arranged, it is symmetrical, offering a good appearance from all sides. An example of the convex curve can be seen in the table arrangement of poinsettias in Color Plate 11.

The "torch" design, a perpendicular (see illustration 5), enables you to fit the shape into a small display area. Many tall flowers, such as the iris with its own spear-shaped foliage, work well here. This is a good shape to use when you have but a few flowers to display. An example of the torch design can be seen in Color Plate 7, the white lilies.

The Hogarth curve or "line of beauty" (see illustration 6) is a particularly graceful looking shape. It is also adaptable for displaying just a few flowers. There are several dried and processed materials such as eucalyptus or magnolia leaves which can be reinforced with wire so they will retain the "S" curve. Then you may fill in the design with your fashioned blossoms.

Illustration 6
Hogarth Curve

Now that you are familiar with some of the most elementary arrangement shapes, consider some of the suitable dried and processed materials available to complement your flowers. There are many materials which can serve both as fillers and as line material with which to establish the framework of the shape your arrangement will take. Two of my favorite materials are eucalyptus and baby's breath. Eucalyptus can be found in colors from beautiful gray to green to all shades of browns and dark reds. (The eucalyptus is shown in Color Plate 12.) It is available in floral shops and in some hobby stores. It can be used either to establish the line of your arrangement or as a filler. It adds a bonus to your fashioned bouquet — a nice fragrance. Baby's breath, dried, can usually be found in the same places you would find eucalyptus. It comes in bundles and is difficult to separate without breakage and waste. Before you separate it, submerge the whole bundle in a tub of warm water and leave it until it will relax enough to part without damage. Actually, when I can, I like to buy fresh baby's breath, place it in the arrangement and let it dry that way. Tendrils and branches from wisteria vine make excellent materials for establishing a shape, especially in a line arrangement. A good example of its use in this manner can be seen in Color Plate 5.

Science sees signs;
Poetry the thing signified.

HARE

The "money plant" or "silver dollar," as it is sometimes called, is an interesting plant to use with fashioned flowers. You can identify it by the silvery pearly discs on each branch. There are several varieties of ferns which are attractive including a white bleached frond and a leather-leaf which comes in both green and a rich brown. Beyond these, there is an endless list of roadside grasses and farmland plants which are beautiful arranged with fashioned flowers. Sage, yucca, oats, wheat, broom-weeds (spray them any color you like), and the bois d'arc apples, sometimes called "hedge apples" or "osage orange," are lovely. (To use the bois d'arc apples, slice rather thin and bake slowly in the oven. Then attach each piece to a wire stem.) And, finally, there are all kinds of pods, seeds, acorns, etc., which can be impaled on a wire and used effectively.

The term "mechanics," as used in this art form, may be foreign to you. In this sense, "mechanics" are those physical properties which serve to control the flowers you are arranging, those which keep them in place, stationary. There are several types of mechanical aids available for arranging both fresh and fashioned flowers. Those of you who are experienced in this field are no doubt familiar with them and have your favorite method of anchoring your posies. For the beginner, I think it is most practical simply to suggest the use of styrofoam.

Styrofoam is readily available in both green and white at most hobby,

floral or variety stores. It comes in rather large sheets and can be cut with a serrated knife to fit any container. In variety stores there are also small pieces available which have been already treated with an adhesive by which you can anchor them to your vases. The chances are, however, that you will use styrofoam without the adhesive backing, holding it in place with any of several brands of fine adhesive material. Pull off what you need, roll it into a snake, put it around the bottom of the styrofoam, and press it into the vase. Be sure there is contact between the styrofoam and the vase so it will stay put.

Rocks, gravel, and sand will come in handy if you are working with a deep vase, a churn, a pitcher, or one of the baskets which make great containers. With these you will be making large arrangements and the container needs to be weighted so it will not easily tip over. For years, I have used a simple method for arranging flowers, one I came across in a magazine. I simply go to a sandpile—and if you have children, you must have a sandpile nearby—and fill a bowl, particularly if it is an opaque one, with sand. Pour water on it until it is damp and set your flowers. The sand will harden enough to keep flowers in their appointed places.

Before inserting your flowers into the arrangement, regardless of what you are using to hold them, spread over the mechanics a coarse material called sphagnum moss. This material gives a neater flower arrangement. Pebbles spread over the top can also give a nice finish for some flowers.

I rather suspected from the beginning that this would be my "If, But, and However" chapter and I have not missed by far. "If I were an expert flower arranger . . . " "However, take these few guidelines and learn by doing . . ." This is the way it is, you see. These are the essentials, some starting points for you to "learn by doing." Container, shape, mechanics, these plus a bit of serendipity are the fundamentals. They might even be compared to "self-reverence, self-knowledge, and self-control" which Tennyson said will lead you to achieve the impossible. These three basics you can learn. The serendipity is your contribution. Serendipity, the gift of finding valuable results not envisioned, comes when you apply your blend of taste, design, initiative. It comes from confidence in yourself.

Many years ago, because of my love of flowers, I joined a garden club. My interest was directed primarily toward the horticultural. Fortunately, however, a good portion of the activities involved instruction in flower arranging. I was terrified! How did I ever get into this impossible situation? Then, to add to my panic, I learned I was expected to enter an arrangement in competition. Me? You've got to be kidding! All I knew about was buttercups and wild flowers. Wild flowers! Suddenly I remembered the vacant lot next door to the school where I took my son each day. Several times lately I had sat

Be it jewel or toy,
Not the prize gives the joy
But the striving to win the prize.
CAXTON

in the warm spring sunshine waiting for the bell to ring and watching a gentle breeze make patterns in the waves of creamy seed puffs stemming from the milkweed in the vacant lot. I wondered now if I could use those intricate puffs. Was it possible they could be something more than a public nuisance? A flower arrangement, maybe? The next day after I dropped my son off at school, I proceeded onto the lot. With courage in one hand and a can of hair spray in the other, I marched to those milkweeds, ignoring the stares of the other mothers depositing their children. With the spray I proceeded to "stabilize" the puffy delicate balls of seed. Then I carefully cut an armload of the weeds, took them to the car, and drove home. With a few "guidelines" from a previously unused book, *Better Homes & Gardens Flower Arranging*, I managed to get those milkweed pods to stay in place long enough to win a blue ribbon! Nice! But what I really won that day was a big batch of confidence. That confidence led me into flower making ". . . so elegant an employment."

. . . Flower making . . . so elegant an employment.

GODEY'S LADY'S BOOK, 1847

Talent, defined, is "the natural endowments of a person." Notice that its definition is not "a person who is gifted with the ability to sing, dance, paint, write, act, etc." We all are created to be creative but we must be inspired to develop our talents. Our world would be static save for those creative talents put into action daily. In the classroom, a "naturally endowed" teacher creatively instructs a group of wiggling children. On a greasy driveway, a young boy creatively improves the "hum" of a motor. And in a spotless kitchen, Mom considers entering a contest with her own recipe for a super soufflé. Her soufflé was the result of an idea and the risk of trying it. All she had to lose was a few eggs and a little spinach. Even a loss could be turned to a rather creative dinner for "Patch" the cat.

I suspect you may be "naturally endowed" in the art of making flowers, else you would not have been interested in this book. Perhaps you will develop this talent and make an even better buttercup. Personal note to first time "losers." Cats don't like buttercups. I've tried it.

Index to Flowers

Alphabetical by Flower Name

206